First Names

FROM ABBY TO ZACH

BY DEBBY FELDER & DANIEL BURT

SCHOLASTIC INC.

New York Toronto London Auckland Sydney Tokyo

**To our parents,
who named us**

Hand-lettering front and back cover: Joanie Ferrara

ISBN 0-590-31307-X

12 11 10 9 8 7 6 5 4 3 2   11   3 4 5 6 7/8

Printed in the U.S.A.   **28**

A

Aaron (Hebrew). Aaron means "lofty" or "high mountain." So if you like heights, you are well named! Aaron also means "inspired." The first high priest of Israel was named Aaron. Other famous Aarons: Aaron Burr, who fought a duel with Alexander Hamilton; baseball's Hall-of-Famer Hank Aaron; and Haroun (Aaron) al-Raschid, hero of the *Arabian Nights* stories.

Abigail, Abby (Hebrew). In the Bible, Abigail means "my father is joy"—an attitude any parent would like. Very soon, the name came to mean "serve with joy" and "source of joy." Abby and **Gail** are nicknames for Abigail and are also popular first names. Abigail Adams was a famous First Lady; Dear Abby gives advice through her newspaper column.

Abraham (Hebrew). If your name is Abraham, you might have many children someday; the name means "exalted father" or "father of multitudes"! The best known Abraham, Abraham Lincoln, did not have many children, but he was a famous and exalted American president. Favorite nicknames are Abe, Abie, and Ham.

Ada. Besides being a palindrome (spelled the same backward and forward), this name is a popular one and has several meanings. In German, the name means "happy"; in the Bible, it means "beauty"; and in Latin, it means "noble birth." A good name all around.

Adam (Hebrew). If you are Adam, you have the world's oldest name; it is said to have belonged to the first man on Earth. According to the Bible, Adam was created from red earth; and so the name means "red" or "man of red earth." It also means "mortal," "human," and "humankind," since the first Adam started the human race. Famous Americans with last names that come from Adam are: Samuel Adams, a patriot; John Adams and John Quincy Adams, presidents; and Jane Addams, a pioneer social worker.

Adela, **Adele**, **Adelia**, **Adelaide**, **Adeline** (German). These various forms of an ancient German name all mean "noble" or "of noble birth" or "noble serpent." So your name grants you wisdom as well as nobility, since the serpent is considered wise! A popular nickname is Addie.

Adrian, Adriana, Adrienne (Latin, Greek). Your name means "rich," "black," and "one from Adria." Believe it or not, all these meanings are related. Adria, an ancient seaport on the Adriatic Sea, had black sand shores and was so rich and famous that the sea was named for it. The Adriatic Sea route brought riches and fortune to other cities, too, and so the name has come to mean "good fortune." The French girls' name, Adrienne, means "dark one from the southern sea." Six popes and a famous Hollywood dress designer were named Adrian.

Agatha (Greek). "Good and kind" are the meanings of this name, more popular in England than America. Aggie is a favorite nickname. Agatha Christie was a favorite English mystery writer.

Agnes (Latin). Like Agatha, Agnes was the name of a saint; it means "purity." In Spanish, the name becomes **Inez**. A great name in the movies and in theater was actress Agnes Moorehead. A famous choreographer is Agnes de Mille.

Aileen—see Eileen.

Alan, Allen, Allan, Allyn, Allain (Celtic). A favorite name in England, Ireland, France, and Greece, as well as in America. In ancient Britain, Alan meant "harmony"; in Ireland, "handsome"; in France, "cheerful"; and in Greece, "a lute player." Like Allan-a-Dale of Robin Hood's merry band, Alans are in harmony wherever they go—even in space, where astronaut Alan Shepard was the first American to orbit the earth. **Alana, Aline,** and **Lana** are girls' names that come from Alan; they mean "light and buoyant" as well as "handsome."

Albert, **Alberta** (German). Princes and dukes favor this name, probably because it means "noble" and "bright." Alberta is the name for girls. When a noble German, Prince Albert, married England's Queen Victoria, he became so popular, he had a coat and a cigar named after him. Albert Einstein was a brilliant scientist and mathematician. And fifteen-year-old Albert Sadacca created brightness—he invented Christmas tree lights! Al and Bert are common nicknames.

Alexander (Greek). This famous and powerful name means "to protect" and "to defend" and "helper of mankind." It has been a favorite with kings, czars, popes, and other famous men. The greatest Alexander of all time was Alexander the Great, who conquered most of the ancient world. He also founded Alexandria and made it a city of great culture and learning. Alexander Graham Bell invented the telephone. With his lightning fastball, Sandy (Alexander) Koufax pitched himself into baseball's Hall of Fame. Nicknames are Alex or Alec, Al, Sandy, and Lex.

Alexandra, **Alexis, Alix** (Greek). All these fine names come from Alexander and mean "a protector" or "a helper of mankind." Queen Alexandra of England was a famous beauty and made the name popular. St. Alexis was a favorite saint in Russia. Pet names are Sandy or **Sandra,** now a popular first name.

Alfred (German or English). This ancient and noble name means "elf," and also "keen counselor" and "wise helper." Long ago, elves were thought to be wise, magical beings who guided men's fortunes. Nicknames are

Al, Alf, Alfie, and Fred. Alfred Nobel invented dynamite and also funded the world-famous Nobel Peace Prize. Alfred the Great was an early Anglo-Saxon king who saved England from a Viking takeover. You already know about Alfred E. Newman of *Mad* magazine, and Alfred Hitchcock, the late, great film director of suspense thrillers.

Alice, Alicia, Alissa, Alyce, Alys, Alyse (Greek). If you're an Alice, you can tell no lies, because your name means "truthful." It also means "nobility." Nicknames are Al, Allie, and Ali. The most famous Alice visited Wonderland by falling down a rabbit hole, and she had a really hare-y time getting home again! Ali McGraw is a famous model turned movie star.

Aline—see Alan.

Alison, Allison (Scottish). Whether you are a boy or a girl, your name means "famous warrior." The name first arrived in Scotland from ancient Rome as **Aloysius** (Al-o-wish-us), a man's name. The early girls' version of this was **Aloyse.** The Scots finally changed that to Alison, and it's been popular this way ever since. In Spanish, Alison means "a sweet-smelling white flower." Other forms of your name are **Aloysia** and **Aloys,** and a nice nickname is Alie.

Amanda, Amy (Latin). Strange as it may seem, Amanda and Amy both mean the same things. Both names mean "to love," "fit to be loved," and "beloved friend." In fact, "amy" is the legal word for friend. In France, the word for friend is *ami,* and a girls' name there is **Aimée.** Amanda has been the name of many romantic heroines in stories; nicknames are Manda and Mandy.

Amelia (Latin). Your name originally came from the name **Emily.** It means "industrious" and "hardworking," and also "golden-tongued flatterer." So if you like giving compliments and working hard, you're not only well named but you've found a sure formula for success! Nicknames are Milly, Millie, Melia, and Mellie. Amelia Earhart was the first woman pilot to fly over the Atlantic Ocean alone.

Andrew, Andrea (Greek). "Strong," "courageous," and also "manly" are the meanings of Andrew and Andrea, popular names in many countries of the world. In France, Andrew becomes **André** (boys) or **Andrée** (girls). The most common nickname for Andrew is Andy, although President Andrew Jackson's nickname was "Old Hickory." Andrew Carnegie founded and funded the Carnegie Foundation. Court jesters, who had the risky job of trying to make kings laugh, were sometimes called "merry andrews."

Angela (Greek). You're an angel—if your name is Angela! This name actually comes from the Greek word *angelos* meaning "a messenger." The archangel, St. Michael, was a heavenly messenger. So it used to be that any child born around the Feast of St. Michael would be named Angel. Other girls' names meaning "angel" are **Angelica** and **Angelina.** Boys' names are spelled **Angelos, Angelo,** or **Angele.** A popular nickname for all these angels is Angie. One of the greatest painters of all time was Michaelangelo. Angie Dickinson and Angela Lansbury are actresses.

nn, Anna, Anne (Hebrew). No matter how you spell it, "grace" and "truth" are the meanings of your name. Originally it came from **Hannah,** a very popular name in colonial times. There are many different forms of the name Ann: **Anabelle, Annabella, Nan, Nancy, Nana, Nina, Annette, Nanette, Ana, Anya, and Anita** (little Ann). A favorite nickname is Annie, made famous by the play and movie about Orphan Annie. Anna Mary Robertson was a painter you may know as Grandma Moses. There were six Queen Annes and now a Princess Anne of England. Annie Oakley was a world-famous sharpshooter of the Old West; Ann Landers is famous for her newspaper advice column.

nthony, Antonia, Antoinette (Latin). These are among the all-time great names; they mean "greatly esteemed," "praiseworthy," and "priceless." In ancient Rome, the name was **Antonius;** in modern Italy it's **Antonio;** in France, **Antoine;** in Poland and Russia, **Anton.** A pretty queen who lost her head in France was Marie Antoinette. A favorite nickname for boys and girls is Tony; girls like Toni as well.

pril (Latin). This lovely name is also the name of the fourth month in the year, the first full month of spring. So it's not surprising that the name April also means "spring." The French spelling of April is **Avril**, also a popular girls' name. Boys are sometimes named **Averill,** as in Averill Harriman, a former ambassador and governor of New York State.

7

rlene, Arlen (Irish). Arlene is a favorite name in Ireland; Arlen is usually a boys' name. There are many different spellings for Arlene—**Arleen, Arline, Arleyne, Arleta,** even **Erline**—and they all mean "a pledge."

rnold (German). Power and strength are yours if your name is Arnold. It means "mighty as an eagle." Nicknames are Arnie and Arno. Arnold Bennett was a famous English writer; Benedict Arnold is considered an American traitor.

rthur (Celtic). Be proud if this is your name because it means "noble," "exalted," and "firm as a rock." Courage and strength are also yours because Arthur has another meaning: "like a bear." Nicknames are Art, Artie, and Arty. The most famous Arthur of all time was King Arthur, who headed the Knights of the Round Table.

udrey (German). Meaning "the noble one" or "of noble strength," Audrey is the name of a saint and also a famous actress, Audrey Hepburn. The word Audrey may stem from the same ancient Anglo-Saxon name that Ethel did—**Athelththryth!**

B

Barbara, Barbra (Greek). Your pretty and popular name comes, believe it or not, from the word "barbarian," and means "strange" or "foreign." When the ancient Greeks heard foreigners speak in languages they couldn't understand, they called it "baa-baa." From this came the word "barbarian," and later, the name Barbara. Famous Barbaras: Barbara Frietchie, who defended the Union flag during the Civil War; Barbra Streisand, a well-known singer-actress; and the Barbie doll.

Barney, Barnaby (Hebrew). Both names are shortened forms of the name **Barnabas,** which means "son of prophecy or consolation." Barney is the version most often seen nowadays, though. Barn is a favorite nickname. A long-running TV series was the popular *Barney Miller.*

Barry (Irish). You have a straight, up-front name if this is yours. Barry means "looking straight at the mark," "marksman," or "spear." Barry was originally a nickname for **Barnard** but has now become popular as a first name. A well-known Barry today is the singer and composer Barry Manilow.

Beatrice (Latin). The ancient Romans invented this name. Beatrice means "a bringer of joy" or "she who blesses or makes happy." Some favorite nicknames are Trixie, Trix, Bea, and Bee. The French spelling, **Beatrix,** is popular here, too. Ramona Quimby's sister is Beatrice, better known as Beezus in Beverly Cleary's stories. Beatrix Potter wrote *A Tale of Peter Rabbit.*

Benjamin (Hebrew). You are very lucky if this popular name is yours, because it means "fortunate." In the Bible, Benjamin was the youngest and favorite son of Jacob's twelve children, so the name also means "son of my right hand" and "son of my strength." Nicknames are Ben, Benny, and Benji. Benjamin Franklin was a VIP (Very Important Person) in the early days of America. He invented the Franklin stove, started public libraries, and helped to found our nation.

Bernard (German). Your name means "bear's heart" or "resolute commander." Favorite nicknames are Bernie or Barney. Girls' names that come from Bernard are **Bernadette** and **Bernardine.** St. Bernard, a monk during the tenth century, founded a famous hospice for travelers at an Alpine pass. St. Bernards are big, protective dogs, originally bred and trained at this hospice to rescue lost travelers.

Bernice, **Berenice** (Greek). What does this ancient name have in common with Victoria? Victory! Bernice is today's version of the ancient Greek name, **Berenike,** which means "a bringer of victory (*nike*)." Nicknames are Bern and Bernie.

Beryl (Greek). You are a real jewel if you are named for the precious, blue-green gemstone called beryl. Your name also means "crystal" or "crystal clear" and is a name shared by both girls and boys.

Bess—see Elizabeth.

Beth (Hebrew). Once a nickname for Elizabeth, Beth has gained great popularity on its own. One meaning is "daughter of God"; another is "house" or "house of joy." There will always be joy in your house if you are named Beth! Some old-fashioned spellings of your name are **Bethel, Bethia, Bethiah, Betya,** and **Bithia.** A famous Beth was gentle Beth March in *Little Women.*

Betsy, Betsey, Bette, Betty, Bettina—see Elizabeth.

Beverly, **Beverley** (Old English). This name is given to boys as well as girls, especially in England. It is a "place name." Literally, it means "dweller at the beaver's lea or meadow." Beverly Sills is a former opera singer. Beverly Cleary is a popular author of stories about Ramona, Henry Huggins, and Ralph the motorcycle mouse.

Bonnie (Latin). Although it sounds as Scots as heather, this name actually comes from the Latin word meaning good (*bona*). But the Scots really give the name its full meaning: A bonnie lass is one who is sweet, pretty, graceful, and good.

Brenda, Brendan (Old Norse). First the name was Brand. Then this boys' name became popular in Ireland as Brendan. Brenda is the feminine version, and both names mean "sword," "burning log," or "fiery." People named Brenda or Brendan are likely to be lively, fiery-tempered, and full of initiative—like St. Brendan of Ireland, who is supposed to have sailed across the Atlantic Ocean long before Columbus. Did St. Brendan discover America first?

Bret, Brett (Celtic). Your name means "a Breton," or "one who comes from Brittany." (Brittany is a region of France.) Brett used to be mostly a boys' name, but it's become a favorite girls' name, too.

Brian, Bryan (Irish). "Strength" and "nobility" are yours if Brian is your name! Brian also means "mighty leader" because of the legendary Irish hero and king, Brian Boru, who won fame in many battles with raiding Vikings.

Bridget (Irish). Your pretty name means "the mighty," or "high," or "strength." St. Bridget of Ireland, known for her goodness, charity, and justice, was the most popular saint of Ireland. In Sweden, you might be called **Brigit** or **Birgit**; in France, **Brigitte**. Nicknames are Birdie, Biddy, Bridgie, Bride, or Bridie.

Brook, **Brooke** (Old English). This place name means, not surprisingly, "a dweller by the stream." It is popular for both boys and girls and is also a last name. The best-known Brooke today is model Brooke Shields.

Bruce (French). If you're a nature lover, you'll be happy to know that your name means "the woods" and "of the brush." Although it came from France, it is now thought of as a Scots name because of Robert Bruce. This famous Scots Highland chief is the national hero of Scotland.

Caitlin—see Katherine.

Candace, Candice, Candis, Candide, Candida (Greek). Your lovely name means "the fire-white or glowing," and also "pure and candid (honest)." Many Egyptian queens had this name. A favorite nickname is Candy, but here's an amazing fact: Daisy is also a nickname for Candace!

Caren—see Karen.

Carl, Carla, Carlo, Carlos, Carlotta, Carly—see Charles.

Carol, Carole, Caryl (French). If you like to sing, you are well named. Carol means "to sing joyfully and melodiously." A carol is also a joyful song of Christmas and a favorite name for Christmas babies, boys as well as girls. Carol Burnett is a TV and movie comedienne.

Caroline, Carolyn (German). Your name comes from **Charles,** which means "a great man." It also means "valiant and strong." A favorite nickname is Carrie. In the *Little House* series, Laura Ingalls's younger sister is Carrie; her mother is Caroline.

Cass, Cassie, Catherine, Cathy, Cathleen— see Katherine.

Cecilia, Celia (Latin). Both names come from the boys' name **Cecil** and, strangely enough, mean "dim-sighted." Celia, however, which is a shortened form of Cecilia, has a meaning of its own—"heavenly." A tuneful note: St. Cecilia is the patron saint of music! Other versions of your name are **Cecily, Cecely, Celine, Cecile,** and **Celinda.** Nicknames are Cis, Cissie, Cissy, and Sis.

Charles (Latin, German). This ancient name has more variations than almost any other. It means "great man" and "strong and manly." In Latin, the name is **Carolus;** Charles is the German spelling. Many popular names come from Charles: **Carl, Carla, Carlo, Carlos, Carlotta, Carly, Carol, Caroline, Charlotte, Cheryl, Karl,** and **Karla.** Nicknames are Chip, Chick, Chuck, Charlie, and Chas. Prince Charles is heir to the throne of England; Charles Lindbergh was the first man to fly alone across the Atlantic Ocean; Charlie Chaplin was a famous silent-movie comedian.

Cheryl (French). "Cherished" or "the cherished one" are the meanings of this lovely name, which is also related to **Charles.** Another way to spell it is **Sheryl.** A favorite nickname is Cher.

Chester (Latin, Old English). Your name comes from the Latin word *castra,* meaning "camp." When the ancient Romans invaded England, this is what they called their army camps. Another meaning is "dweller in a fortified town." In fact, Lan*chester,* Man*chester,* and Chester are just a few of the modern-day English cities that were once "fortified towns." **Lester** is a closely related name. Chet is the popular nickname.

Christina, Christine (Greek). This popular name comes from **Christos,** the Greek name for Jesus, and means "the Christian" or "an anointed one." **Christie, Christy, Kristin, Kerstin, Kirstin,** and **Christobel** are other forms of your name. Nicknames are Chris, Kris, Chrissie, Tina, and even Tiny. Tennis star Chris Evert Lloyd first won worldwide fame in tournaments when she was only 16 years old.

Christopher (Greek). Your name, which means "a follower of Christ," has been popular since the days of the early Christians. St. Christopher is the patron saint of travelers, and today many people who travel wear Saint Christopher medals. Nicknames are Chris, Kit, and Christy. Christopher Columbus sailed west in 1492 and discovered America. Kit Carson was an American trapper, guide, Indian scout, and explorer.

Claire, Clare, Clara, Clarence, Clarice, Clarissa (Latin). All these names mean "bright and clear." In Italian legends, Saint Clare had the power to see events at a great distance, and when television was invented, she became its patron saint! (The word "television" actually means "seeing at a distance.") Clara Barton was the founder of the American Red Cross, and Clarence Darrow was a famous American defense lawyer.

Claude, Claudette, Claudia, Claudine (Latin). Your name means "the lame one" because of the ancient Roman emperor, Claudius, who had a lame leg. Claudius was one of the most peaceful and just rulers of his time. A nickname for Claude is Claudie. Claude Rains starred in *The Phantom of the Opera* and other popular movies of the 1940s; Claudette Colbert was a favorite movie actress of that era.

Clifford (Old English). If your name is Clifford, do you live near a cliff and a ford (stream)? Even if you don't, it still makes sense that your name means "dweller at the ford near the cliff"! A favorite nickname is Cliff.

Colette—see Nicole.

Conrad (German). Your name has three possible meanings: "helper," "wisdom," or "able in speech and counsel." Two variations of this name are **Curt** and **Kurt**; Con, Connie, and Conny are nicknames.

Constance (Latin). Congratulate yourself if Constance is your name! It means "constant and firm" and "one who perseveres." An important Roman emperor was called Constantine the Great, and the name Constantine is still popular in Greece. Nicknames are Con, Connie, or Connee.

Corey (Irish). Both boys and girls have this "place name"; it means "from the round hill" or "one who dwells by a hollow or misty pool." Corey also means "the closer." Some people like to spell it **Cori** or **Cory**.

Cornelia, Cornelius. Your name can either mean "war horn" or "horn of the sun" (Latin), or "the cornel tree" (Greek). In ancient Rome, the war horn was a symbol of royalty. The cornel tree is better known in this country as the dogwood. **Cornel** is a shortened version of Cornelius; Corny, Neel, and Neely are nicknames.

Craig (Scottish). In ancient Scotland, if you were named Craig, you usually lived on a "crag," which is a steep, rocky hill or cliff. Today, you may live on flat land or in a twenty-story apartment building, but if your name is Craig it still means "crag dweller." Craig is often a last name, too.

Curt—see Conrad.

Cynthia (Greek). This lovely name means "the moon" or "the moon goddess." In Greek myths, Mount Cynthus was the home of the moon goddess, Artemis, who became known as "the Cynthian." Favorite nicknames are Cyn, Cyndie, and Cindy. The English Channel (between England and France) has challenged many long-distance swimmers; the first and fastest swimmer ever to complete a *double* crossing (from one shore to the other and back) was nineteen-year-old Cindy Nicholas.

D

Daisy (English). In any garden of names, Daisy really stands out! Your name means "the day's eye" because of a daisy's golden, sunlike center and bright, white petal-lashes. Daisy used to be a nickname for Candace and Margaret, but now it is popular on its own.

Dale (German). This nice, short name has a short meaning and a long one. You can choose between "dweller in the dale" or "a dweller in a vale or valley between hills." Either way, Dale is a popular first name for both boys and girls. It is often a last name as well.

Dana (Scandinavian). Both boys and girls have this name. It means "a Dane" (someone who comes from Denmark) and also "bright and pure as day." Dana is also a family (last) name. Dana Wynter is a television and movie star. Richard Henry Dana wrote a famous book called *Two Years Before the Mast.*

Daniel, Daniela, Daniele (Hebrew). Your name means "a judge" or "God has judged." In the Bible, the prophet Daniel was thrown into a den of lions for refusing to give up his religion. Amazingly, he escaped unharmed. Nicknames are Dan and Danny. Daniela and Daniele are the feminine forms of the name. Daniel Webster was a famous American lawyer and orator. Daniel Boone was an early American frontiersman.

Darlene (English). "The tenderly beloved" or "darling" are two meanings of this pretty name. Another way to spell it is **Darline; Daryl** is the boys' version.

David (Hebrew). Your popular name originally meant "beloved" or "darling," and then "friend" and "beloved one." In the Bible, David was a shepherd boy who killed the giant, Goliath. David was also a musician; most of the psalms are his own songs. He was very wise as well as gifted, and became one of Israel's greatest kings. Nicknames are Dave, Davy, and Davey. In Wales, some Davids are nicknamed Taffy! Davy Crockett was an American frontiersman.

Dawn (Latin). This lovely name is a translation of the Latin name for the dawn goddess, **Aurora,** and means "the awakening." Other dawn names are **Zora** (Arabic); **Gwawr** (Welsh); **Aurore** (French); and **Roxanne** (Persian). The princess in *The Sleeping Beauty,* who slept for one hundred years, was named Aurora.

Dean, **Deane** (Old English). Your name means "from the valley or dene." Another possible meaning is "leader or head of a school or church." Today, heads of colleges are called deans. A nickname for Dean is Dino.

Deanna—see Diana.

Deborah, **Debra, Debora, Devora** (Hebrew). Your popular name actually means "a bee." And, because of a bee's humming sound, it has come to mean "eloquence in speech." But there's more—your name also means "she rules" and "queen bee" because of Queen Deborah, a famous warrior and prophet in the Bible. Deborah was a favorite name among the New England Puritans. Nicknames are Debby, Debbie, and Deb. Debbie Reynolds and Deborah Kerr are two famous movie stars. During the Revolutionary War, Deborah Sampson wanted to join the fight so much, she dressed as a man and enlisted in the army!

Deirdre (Irish). Your pretty name means "the raging one." It also means "sorrow" because of Ireland's most famous queen, Deirdre. Beautiful Deirdre led such an unhappy life that she became known as the "Queen of Sorrows." But today Deirdre is simply one of the nicest names anybody can have! **Dorcas** is another form of your name; Dedee and Dee are nicknames.

Delores, **Dolores** (Latin). Your pretty name is popular in Spanish-speaking countries around the world. It originally comes from the word *dolor,* which means "grief" or "sorrow." It became as popular a name as Mary or Maria because Mary, the mother of Jesus, is sometimes known as "Our Lady of Sorrows" *(dolores)*. Nicknames are Lola, Lolita, and Lo. **Lola** and **Lolita** are also first names.

Denise, Denis, Dennis, Denys (Greek). All these names call for a celebration—and a little playacting! They all come from the name of the Greek god **Dion** or **Dionysius,** the god of wine and drama. (Greek drama grew out of the noisy festivals of Dionysius.) Nicknames for Dennis are Denny or Dion.

Diana, Diane, Dianne, Dian, Diahnn, Dyan (Latin). When the moon shines, it can sometimes be as "bright as day"—and that's exactly what your name means! In Roman mythology, Diana was the moon goddess and also the goddess of forests and animals. **Deanna** and **Dionna** are other versions of your name. A favorite nickname is Di. Diana Ross is an actress and singer who started her career as lead singer of the Supremes. Beautiful Princess Diana is married to Prince Charles, heir to the British throne.

Dominic, Dominick (Latin). Were you born on Sunday? It used to be that boys born on Sunday, the Lord's day *(domine),* were given this name; it means "belonging to the Lord." In Spain, boys might be called **Domingo;** in France, girls are sometimes called **Dominique.** In olden England, those who were lucky enough to own land were called "dominics" or "doms," which means "master." Dom is a favorite nickname for Dominic, and Dom DeLuise is known for his crazy antics in the movies and on TV.

Donald (Celtic). Your name means "world ruler" and "prince of the universe." Another meaning is "proud chief." And the MacDonald (son of Donald) clan is one of the oldest in Scotland. In England, Donald is sometimes spelled **Donal;** in Ireland, it's **Dommall, Donnell, Donally,** or **Donley.** Nicknames are Don, Donnie, and Donny. College professors in England are called "dons." In Spain, it is a title of respect. Donald J. Sobol writes stories about Encyclopedia Brown, the amazing boy detective. The only pitcher in baseball ever to pitch a perfect game in the World Series was former Yankee Don Larsen.

Donna (Latin). You can expect some respect if Donna is your name! It means "a lady," and it has been a favored name with Italian nobility since ancient Roman days. In fact, "madonna" means "my lady." In Spain, Doña is used as a title of respect before women's names. Girls born on Sunday are sometimes called Donna.

Dora, Dorothy (Greek). These pretty names come from **Theodora,** which came from **Theodore,** a boys' name. Both Dora and Dorothy mean "God's gift" or simply "a gift." Variations of Dorothy are: **Dorothea, Doreen, Dorinda, Dortha, Feodora, Thea,** or **Theda.** Nicknames are Dotty, Dolly, and Dodi, which also means "beloved," and even Dodo! Dolly Madison was an early First Lady who was the first to serve ice cream at the White House. Dorothy Gale rode a cyclone to Oz in *The Wizard of Oz.*

Doris (Greek). Your name means "a Dorian girl" or "of the Doric people." The Dorians were early Greeks who lived in the Doris mountain range. If you like the beach, you'll be happy to know that your name also means "of the sea." In Greek mythology, Eldoris was the mother of fifty beautiful sea nymphs. Other forms of your name are **Dorris** and **Dory**. A famous acting Doris is Doris von Kappelhoff, who changed her name to Doris Day!

Douglas (Celtic). Your name is popular as both a first and last name. It means "dark blue" and "from the black stream" because of the dark waters of the Douglas River in Scotland. The area around this river was where the great Douglas clan, or family, lived. In ancient Scotland, even the girls were sometimes named Douglas! Nicknames are Doug, Dougie, Dug, and Duggie. Douglas Fairbanks was a movie star of silent adventure movies; he insisted on doing dangerous feats himself—without a stunt man substitute. Have you ever heard of "Wrong-way Corrigan"? He was Douglas Corrigan, an early aviator who was the first person to fly from California to New York in less than twenty-eight hours. In 1939, this was quite a feat. But when Corrigan started on his return trip back to California, he accidentally got lost and ended up flying in the opposite direction. He flew across the Atlantic Ocean and landed in Ireland!

Dyan—see Diane.

E

Earl, Earle, Errol (English). Your old and honored name means "nobleman or chief." Another meaning is "chief of keen intelligence." Earls, like dukes, were usually members of the nobility. Titles like these are rare nowadays, but some countries, like England, still use them. **Earline** is the feminine version.

Edith (English). Believe it or not, your name was once spelled **Eadgyth**! Then it was shortened to **Ardith**, before it finally became Edith. However you spell it, yours is a lucky name and means "rich, happy, and prosperous." Some variations of your name are **Edyth**, **Editha**, **Eda**, and **Dita**. A favorite nickname is Edie. Edith Nesbit wrote children's stories to support her five children, so it won't surprise you to hear that one story is called *Five Children and It*.

Edward (English). If your name is Edward, count yourself lucky. You have one of the most popular, as well as one of the oldest and most honored names around! It means "rich" and "guardian of prosperity" and was the name of many kings of England. In France, it's **Edouard**; in Germany, **Eduard**; in Norway, **Audvard** or **Jaward**. Nicknames are Ed, Eddy, Eddie, Ted, Teddy, Bud, Buddy, Ned, and Neddy. Famous Edwards: Ed Sullivan, a former TV variety show host who brought the Beatles to American TV, and Eddie Jaedel, the shortest man ever to become a major-league baseball player. Jaedel was three feet seven inches tall and played with the former St. Louis Browns.

Eileen (Irish). Your name is one of many that originally came from the name **Helen**. Eileen is a really popular name in Ireland as well as in this country, and it means "light," "bright," and "pleasant." Other ways to spell your name are **Aileen** and **Ilene**.

Elaine, Elain, Elayne (Greek, Welsh). Your name comes from **Helen** and means "bright" and "light"; its Welsh meaning is "a fawn." **Lainie** is a pretty nickname as well as a name on its own. In the King Arthur stories, Elaine, the Lily Maid of Astolot, fell fatally in love with the queen's own knight, Sir Lancelot.

Eleanor, Eleanore, Elinor, Ellinor (Greek). This name comes from **Helen** too, and means "light" and "bright." Other variations of Eleanor are **Elnora, Eleonora, Leonna, Lenore, Leonora,** and **Lena**. Ellie and Nora are two favorite nicknames, and **Nora** is often a name on its own. Eleanor Roosevelt was a famous First Lady who traveled around the country and the world, representing her husband. Later, she became a U.N. adviser.

Eli, Elias, Eliot, Elliot (Hebrew). All these names stem from Eli, which means "Jehovah is God" and "the highest." Eli Whitney is known for his famous invention, the cotton gin. Eli Wallach is an actor.

Elizabeth (Hebrew). Are you an Elizabeth—or are you a **Beth, Bess, Betsy, Betsey, Bette, Betty, Elsie, Eliza, Lizzie, Liza, Liz, Libby, Lissa,** or **Lisa?** These names are actually nicknames for Elizabeth but have also become very popular as names on their own. Your name comes from the Bible and means "oath of God" and "house of joy." Other forms of your name are **Elissa, Elspeth, Bettye, Lisbeth, Lisabet,** and **Lisabeth.** In France, you might be called **Babette** or **Elise;** in Germany, **Ilse;** in Italy, **Bettina.** Famous Elizabeths: Elizabeth I of England was queen in the days of Raleigh, Drake, and Shakespeare. She beat the Spanish, encouraged exploration, and was known as "Good Queen Bess." Today, England is ruled by good Queen Elizabeth II. Elizabeth Taylor is a famous actress; Betsy Byars is a well-known author.

Ellen (Scottish). This variation of **Helen** really shines on its own! It means "light" and "bright" and was a popular name in Scotland long before it became a favorite in this country. **Elin, Elyn,** and **Ellyn** are other pretty ways to spell it.

Elnora—see Eleanor.

Eloise—see Louisa.

Elroy—see Leroy.

Emily, Emilia (Latin). If your name is Emily, you probably like to get right to work, because your name means "the industrious one." And if you like to talk things over first, you'll be happy to know that Emily also means "golden tongued" or "a flatterer." In France and Germany, your name is spelled **Amalie.** The names **Amelia** and **Emeline** come from this name, too. Nicknames are Em and Emmy. Emily Dickinson was a famous American poet; Emily Post taught our grandparents perfect manners.

Emma (German). Your pretty name means "one who heals." It also means "honored ancestor" or "grandmother." *Ammas* (grandmothers) were especially honored by their families in Germany. Emma Willard founded the first U.S. Women's College in 1821. Emma Edmonds was a spy in the American Civil War; she posed as a soldier and a farmhand and was never caught.

Enid (Celtic). This pretty name means "the soul or spirit." Enid the Good was one of the heroines in the King Arthur stories. In fact, it used to be that the highest praise any woman could receive was to be called "a second Enid."

Eric, Erica (Old Norse, German). Hold your head high if this is your name! It means "kingly" and "ruler," and also "ever powerful" and "regal." The flame-haired Viking seaman, Eric the Red, discovered Greenland. His son, Leif Ericson, is said to have discovered America many years before Christopher Columbus. Erica is a very popular girls' name in Germany; **Erich** is the boys' name. Nicknames for Eric are Rick, Rickie, and Ricky. Nicknames for Erica are Rickie and Rikki. Erich Weiss became the most famous magician of all time. You know him as Harry Houdini.

Erin (Irish). "Peace" is yours if Erin is your name. Erin means "peace" and is also the ancient name for Ireland (now called Eire). So, another meaning of your name is "girl from Ireland." Other ways to spell your name are **Erinn** and **Erina**.

Erline—see Arlene.

Ernest, Ernst (German). Not surprisingly, Ernest means "sincere" or "intent in purpose"—in other words, earnest! Another meaning is "an eagle." Favorite nicknames are Ern and Ernie. Ernest Hemingway was a famous American writer; Ernest Borgnine is an actor known for his tough-guy roles.

Esther, Estelle, Estella, Stella (Latin, Persian, Hebrew). You have real star quality if any of these names are yours; they all stem from **Ishtar,** the Persian goddess of love, and they all mean "star." Stella is the Latin word for "star"; Estelle is French; Estella is Spanish. In the Bible, the noble Queen Esther risked her life to save her people from being massacred.

Eugene, Eugenia, Eugenie (Greek, Latin). Lucky you, your name means "born lucky," "well-born," and "of noble birth"! So it's not surprising that Eugene has been a popular name of princes, saints, and popes. A favorite nickname is **Gene,** which is also a name on its own. Eugenie is the feminine form of this name. A famous Eugenie was the French Empress Eugenie who was known for her style and extravagance. Gene Tunney was a great boxer who became the world heavyweight champ in 1926. Gene Tierney was a popular actress who starred in the movies, *The Ghost and Mrs. Muir* and *Laura.*

Eva—see Eve.

Evan (Celtic). Your name can mean either "a youth," "a young bowman," or "one who is well born"—take your pick! This name is one of many to come from **John.** Evan is spelled **Ywain** in Wales, where the name is especially popular. Evans is a frequent last name. Dale Evans is an actress; Charles Evans Hughes was a Chief Justice of the U.S. Supreme Court.

Eve (Hebrew). If your name is Eve, you have the first woman's name ever recorded. Your name means "mother of all living" and "life," because Eve was the first woman on earth, according to the Bible. The names **Eva** and **Evelyn** come from this name, too. Popular names for boy and girl twins used to be Adam and Eve. And if you order two poached eggs on toast in a restaurant, don't be surprised if you hear the waitress tell the cook, "Adam and Eve on a raft!" A favorite nickname is Evie.

Evelyn (Hebrew). Your name is an offspring of **Eve** and means "life." In Ireland your name also means "pleasant and agreeable," and may be spelled **Eveleen.** Evvie is a popular nickname. Sometimes men are named Evelyn, most often in England.

F

Faith (Latin). Like Hope and Charity, Faith is a "virtue" name and was popular in the days of the Puritans. It means "the believing or faithful," and also "to trust." **Fay** is a nickname and also a name on its own.

Fay, Faye. This pretty name can either mean "the believing or faithful" (Latin) or "fairy" (Old French). Fay is also a nickname for **Faith.** Famous Fays: In the King Arthur stories, Morgan le Fey was a wicked sorceress; in the first *King Kong* movie, actress Fay Wray played the object of Kong's affections.

Felice, Felica, Felicity (Latin). Whichever way you spell your name, good luck should definitely be yours! All three names mean "the fortunate or happy one" or "the lucky one." Felicitas was the Roman goddess of good luck and was also in charge of the horn of plenty —the symbol of a good harvest. A favorite nickname is Fee. A male version of this name is **Felix,** which also means "happy" and "fortunate." Felix Mendelssohn was a famous composer.

Florence (Latin, Celtic). This name means "flowering or blooming" or "fair child." Also, some children are named for the famous city of Florence, Italy. Florence Nightingale was. She made the name popular when she became the first female British army nurse to go to the war front in the 1800s. Soldiers called her "The Lady with the Lamp." Favorite nicknames for Florence are Flo, Florrie, Floss, and Flossie.

Frances, Francesca, Francine, Francis, Frank, Franklin (German). All these names originally came from an ancient German tribe called the Franks, meaning "the free" or "the freemen." The Franks also gave their name to the country of France. In Germany, boys are **Franz** or **Franck.** In France, it's **François** or **Franchet** (boys) and **Françoise** (girls). Nicknames are Fran, Franny, and Frannie. Frank is also a nickname for Francis and Franklin. Famous Franks: Francis Scott Key, who wrote "The Star-Spangled Banner"; Sir Francis Drake, an English explorer; Franklin D. Roosevelt and Franklin Pierce, two U.S. presidents; and Frank Sinatra, the singer.

Frederic, Frederick, Frederica, Fredericka, Freda, Frieda (German). Your name means "rich," "powerful and peaceful," and "a peaceful ruler." In fact, many German emperors and kings were named Frederick. Like Friday, your name comes from Freya, the German goddess of love and beauty. Nicknames are Fritz, Fritzie, Fred, Freddy, and Freddie. Frederick Barbarossa, emperor of the Holy Roman Empire and a crusader, was known for his flaming red beard and fierce ways; Fred Astaire is a dashing dancer and a movie star.

G

Gabriel, Gabriella, Gabrielle (Hebrew). Your name means "a man of God" and "God's strong man." In the Bible, the Archangel Gabriel was one of the most important angels, and he is often pictured blowing his heavenly trumpet. Girls are called Gabriella and Gabrielle. Nicknames are Gabe, Gaby, and Gabby.

Gail, Gale (Scandinavian, Irish). If this is your name, you might be "lively" and like to "sing" or "make merry." Some other meanings of your name are "a strong, singing wind," "a ravine," or "a stranger." Gale is both a boys' and girls' name, and can also be spelled **Gaile, Gael,** or **Gayle.** It is sometimes a nickname for **Abigail.**

Gary, Garry (German). Your popular name is also a nickname for **Gerald, Gerard,** and **Garrett.** But Gary really stands on its own and means "spear carrier," "spear bearer," or "mighty spear." Gary Cooper was a movie star probably best known for his strong, silent, cowboy roles. His real name was Frank J. Cooper.

Gene—See Eugene.

Geoffrey—See Jeffrey.

George (Greek). Your name means "worker in the earth" or "a farmer," and is truly an honorable one. Many famous people in history have been named George, starting with St. George, the patron saint of England. According to legend, he was the slayer of a terrible, fire-breathing, people-eating dragon. St. George's heroic deeds have made him a symbol of courage and valor. In Spain, your name is **Jorge;** in Scotland, **Geordie;** and in Russia, **Yuri.** A favorite nickname is Georgie. The feminine versions of George are **Georgia, Georgina, Georgeann,** or **Georgette.** George Washington was our first president, and six English kings were also named George. Super slugger Babe Ruth's real name was George Herman Ruth.

Gerald, Gerold, Geraldine (German). In ancient times, Gerald was the name of great warriors and soldiers. Your name means "mighty with a spear" or a "ruler." It also means "a brave warrior." A favorite nickname is Gerry. Gerald Ford is a former U.S. president, but did you know that his real first name is Leslie?

Gilbert (German). Your name means "bright pledge or bright sword." Favorite nicknames are Gil and Bert; two more nicknames you may not know are Gib and Gip.

Gillian—See Julia.

Gina—see Regina.

Ginger—see Virginia.

Gladys (Welsh). "A princess" or "ruler over a territory" are two Welsh meanings of Gladys. The name may be related to *gladiolus,* the sword lily, or *gladius*, sword. Both are Latin words. Some also see a connection between Gladys and **Claudia.** (See **Claudia** for more information.) In Wales, Gladys is spelled **Gwladys.** A favorite nickname is Glad.

Glen, Glenn (Celtic). Glen is a place name, meaning "of the glen" or "of the narrow valley." (In early times, people were named for the place where they lived.) Glen is a popular name in England, Ireland, and Scotland, as well as in this country. Another version of Glen is **Glendon. Glynis** is the feminine form.

Gloria (Latin). "Glory" and "glorious grace" are yours if this is your name! And you can be doubly proud if your name is Gloria, because it also means "to exult in pride and joy." A favorite nickname is Glory. Gloria Swanson was the glamorous star of many silent movies.

Gordon (Old English). Believe it or not, your name means "from the three-cornered hill"! But if there aren't any three-cornered hills near your house, you'll be happy to know that Gordon also means "a hero" or "a strong man." It's popular both as a first and a last name, especially in Scotland, home of the Gordon clan. Your name is sometimes spelled **Gordin.** Favorite nicknames are Gordie and Gordy.

Grace (Latin) You're a lucky girl if your name is Grace because it means "loved, favored, and honored"! Your name also means "divine favor." In the Greek myths, the "three Graces" were beautiful maidens, representing beauty, love, and joy. A favorite nickname is Gracie. One of the greatest heroines in ancient Irish legends was Grace of Ireland. The late Princess Grace of Monaco was Grace Kelly, an American movie star, before she married and became a princess.

Gregory (Greek). "To awaken" or "the vigilant one" are two meanings of your popular name. Another meaning is "the fierce." Many saints and popes have had this name, and the next time you glance at a calendar, think of Pope Gregory XIII—he invented our calendar. It's called the Gregorian calendar in his honor. A favorite nickname is Greg. Gregory Peck is a popular Hollywood actor.

Greta, Gretchen—see Margaret.

Guy (Celtic, Old French, German, Latin). If your name is Guy, you have a variety of meanings to choose from: "sensible," "guide," "warrior," or "life." And, as you know, a "guy" is also a slang word for a boy or man. Guy de Maupassant was a famous French writer.

Gwen, Gwendolyn (Celtic). These pretty names mean "white one," "white wave," or "fair one." They come from **Guinevere,** the name of King Arthur's beautiful queen. In ancient Welsh legends, Gwen was the goddess of love. A full name, it is often short for Gwendolyn. Variations of your name are **Gwynne, Gwyneth,** and **Gwendolen.** Gwennie and Wendy are nicknames; **Wendy** is also a name on its own.

Harold (Old English, German). If your name is Harold, be prepared to take the lead! Your name means "commander" and "to rule." Many kings named Harold were also great warriors, so your name has also come to mean "great in battle." Favorite nicknames are Harry and Hal. Three ancient kings were named Harold Harefoot, Harold Bluetooth, and Harold Fairhair!

Harriet (German). This name means "mistress of the house," and, like **Henrietta,** it is also a feminine form of **Henry. Harriette** and **Harriatta** are other versions of this name; Hattie and Harry are favorite nicknames.

Harry—see Henry.

Heather (Scottish). Your pretty name comes from the rosy purple flowering plant that grows on the moors in Scotland and England; the name means "flowering heath." (A heath is a wild, flat stretch of land). Heather is a really popular name in Scotland and England, and of course, here in this country, too.

Helen, Helene (Greek). You'll light up anybody's life if this is your name! Your name means "a torch," "a light," and "the bright one." Helen of Troy, the most beautiful woman in the ancient world, first made the name popular and gave it the meaning of "fair one." Her beauty drove men to war! Variations of Helen are: **Eleanor, Ellen, Eileen, Elaine,** and **Nora**. **Hélène** is French; **Elena** is Spanish; and **Galina** is Russian for Helen.

Henry, Henrietta (German). Your name has been a longtime favorite of many kings and rulers and means "ruler of private property" and "home ruler." Boys are **Heinrich, Heine,** or **Heinz** in Germany; **Enrico** or **Enzio** in Italy; **Enrique** in Spain. In France, it's **Henriette** (girls) and **Henri** or **Herriot** (boys). Nicknames: Harry, Hal, Hen, and Hank. Henriettas are also called Hallie. Henry Hudson, a Dutch explorer, discovered the Hudson River. There were quite a few kings of England named Henry, but King Henry VIII really stands out. He was known, among other things, for his huge size, his terrible temper, and his six wives!

Herbert (German). Yours is one of many names that were often given to great soldiers—it means "bright army" and "bright warrior." Nicknames are Herb, Herbie, Bert, and Bertie.

Herman (German). This name means "soldier or man of the army." Another meaning is "war man." Herm and Hermie are nicknames.

Hew—see Hugh.

Hilary, Hillary (Latin, Greek). Your pretty name means "the cheerful and merry," and is a boys' name, too. Hillary can also be a last name. Explorer Sir Edmund Hillary was the first man to climb to the top of the highest mountain in the world, Mount Everest.

Hilda (German, Norse). "War maiden" or "battle maiden" are the meanings of this name. In Norse mythology, Hilda was one of the Valkyrs (val-keers), maidens who carried the souls of slain warriors to Valhalla, the Norse heaven. Hil and Hildy are favorite nicknames.

Holly, Hollis (English). The name Holly is as popular as Carol for girls born around Christmastime. Hollis is usually the boys' version. Your name comes from the red-berried, shiny-leaved evergreen that brightens homes at Christmas. Legend has it that holly wreaths gave shelter to the elves who brought good luck to the house; your name really means "good luck."

Howard (German). If your name is Howard, keep a close eye on this fact—your name means "guardian," "watchman," or "warden." Howie is a favorite nickname. Famous Howards include Howard Cosell, the gravel-voiced, talkative sportscaster of radio and TV, and Howard Hughes, who was said to have been the richest man in the world.

Hugh (German). Your name means "mind or intelligence." Other versions of this name are **Hugo, Huey, Hew, Hughes, Hutch**—and **Huggins!** A favorite nickname is Hughie. Victor Hugo was the author of the book *The Hunchback of Notre Dame.*

I

Ida (German). It's a happy fact that this pretty name can mean "happy," "industrious," or "rich." In ancient Greece, Mount Ida was said to be the meeting place of the gods.

Ilene —see Eileen.

Inez —see Agnes.

Ingrid (Scandinavian). Your name originally comes from **Ing,** the Norwegian god of the harvest, peace, and prosperity; Ingrid actually means "Ing's daughter." Two other forms of this name are **Inga** and **Inger. Ingua** was an ancient spelling, and one Ingua was a famous Viking chieftain. Neat nickname: Inky.

Ira (Hebrew). This Biblical name means "the watchful" or "the descendant." In the Bible, Ira was a chief captain in King David's army.

Irene (Greek). Your name means "peace" and comes from **Eirene,** the Greek goddess of peace. Originally, your name was pronounced "eye-ree-nee." Other forms of your name are **Irena, Eirena, Iruna,** and **Irina.** Nicknames are Rennie or Rene.

Iris (Greek). Your name means "a rainbow" because of Iris, the Greek goddess of rainbows. She used to travel on rainbows when she delivered messages to the gods. As everyone knows, rainbows are rare and lovely things, seen only when summer rain and sunshine meet. So color yourself lucky if your name is Iris!

Irving (Celtic). This name stems from **Irvin** and **Irvine;** it means "beautiful," "handsome," and "fair." The names **Mervin, Marvin,** and **Irwin** are related to Irving, but Irwin has a meaning of its own, too: it's "sea friend" and "lover of the sea."

Isabel, Isabella, Isabelle (Hebrew). Your pretty name is related to **Elizabeth** and means "oath of God." Isabel may also have come from the name **Jezebel.** Some nicknames are Izzy, Iz, Nib, Tib, Tibbie, Bel, Bella, and Belle. It was Queen Isabella of Spain who put up the money for Columbus's famous voyage, when he accidentally discovered America!

J

Jack (Hebrew). Jack is a nickname for **Jacob** or **John,** but it is also very popular on its own. Take your pick from two possible meanings: "one who follows after"or "gracious gift of God." (See **Jacob** and **John** for more information.) To show how popular your name really is, here are some common English words: jack (used to lift a car); jack knife; blackjack (game); jackstones; jack-o'-lantern; jacket; and jackpot. Jackie Robinson was the first black baseball player in the major leagues. Jackie Stewart is a famous race-car driver; Jackie Gleason is a zany comedian.

Jacalyn, Jaclyn, Jacklyn—see Jacqueline.

Jacob (Hebrew). Your name means "following after" because of Jacob in the Bible, who was born after his brother, Esau. Jacob was the father of Joseph, who is famous for his multi-colored coat. Jake and Jack are popular nicknames. Jacob Grimm was one-half of the brothers Grimm, who wrote the famous fairy tales. The next time you buy something at a store, think of Jake Ritty. He invented the cash register!

Jacqueline (French). This pretty name means "one who follows after" and comes from **Jacobina** and **Jamesina,** the feminine forms of **Jacob** and **James.** Jacqueline is a popular name in France, and a favorite in this country, too. Other ways to spell it are: **Jacalyn, Jaclyn,** and **Jacklyn.** Jack and Jackie are two favorite nicknames. Jacqueline Kennedy Onassis was a famous First Lady. In 1931, "Jackie" Mitchell became the first professional female pitcher in baseball. She made sports history by striking out the great home-run hitter, Babe Ruth!

James (Hebrew). Many famous people share your name, because James has always been popular. The name comes from **Jacob** and means "one who follows after." James is a favored name in other countries as: **Jacques** (French); **Giacomo,** (Italy); **Diego, Iago,** or **Jaime** (Spain); and **Jacov** (Russia). Neat nicknames are Jim, Jimmie, Jimmy, Jamie, Jem, Jemmy, and, believe it or not, Jimbo! Six U.S. presidents and five kings of Scotland have had your name. Two Jameses of baseball fame are pitchers Jim "Catfish" Hunter and Jim Palmer. Another sports hero is Jim Thorpe, who was not only a great football player but an Olympic champion as well.

Jane, Jayne (Hebrew). Your pretty name means "God's gracious gift." It is a feminine form of **John,** and almost as popular. Janes in Italy are called **Giovanna** or **Gionina;** in Spain, **Juana, Juanita,** or **Nita.** A favorite nickname is Janie. Lady Jane Grey was a queen of England who ruled for nine short days.

Janet (Hebrew). Because your name originally comes from the name **Jane**, it also means "God's gracious gift." **Janette** is another way to spell it, and a neat nickname is **Jan,** which is also a name on its own. The first actress ever to win an Academy Award (an Oscar) was Janet Gaynor, in 1928.

Janice, Janis (Hebrew). Yours is another entry in the **Jane** name game and, like Jane, means "God's gracious gift." But your name has the added meaning of "gracious and merciful." A popular nickname is **Jan,** also an actual first name now. Janis Joplin was a famous rock singer of the '60s.

Jason (Greek). Now a very popular name, Jason comes from a Greek word which means "the healer." The most famous Jason is the hero of a Greek myth. To prove he was the rightful king of Thessaly, Jason had to bring back the beautiful but well-guarded Golden Fleece. He finally did, but not before he and his crew met up with some incredible, mythical monsters! In real life, Jason Robards is an actor. Jase is a neat nickname.

Jean (Hebrew). Like **Janet** and **Janice,** your name comes from **Jane.** This means that you are also "God's gracious gift." In France, your name is **Jeanne** or **Jeanette.** Favorite nicknames are Jeanie and Jeannie. **Jeanine** is a variation of Jean.

Jeffrey, Geoffrey (German, English). Whether you spell it with a *J* or a *G,* it means the same: "God's peace," "gift of peace," and "peace of the land." Your name comes from the German name **Gottfried. Godfrey,** Geoffrey, and Jeffrey are the English versions. Jeff, Jeffy, and Geoff are nicknames.

Jennifer (Celtic). Jennifer means "the white or fair one" or "fair lady." Today, it is one of the most popular girls' names in this country. Jennifer came from **Guinevere,** went to France and became **Genevieve,** then came back to England in its present form, Jennifer. Nicknames are Jenny, Jen, and Jennie. Jenny Lind was a popular singer in the 1800s. She came from Sweden and was known as the "Swedish Nightingale." Jennifer Jones is an actress.

Jeremy, Jeremiah (Hebrew). Both names mean "exalted of the Lord" and "God will uplift" because of the great Biblical prophet, Jeremiah. In fact, a jeremiah has come to mean a prophet—someone who can foretell the future. Jeremy is a shortened version of Jeremiah; the name became popular in this country during the 1700s. A favorite nickname is Jerry.

Jerome (Greek and Latin). Jerome means "the holy or sacred name." It was originally spelled **Hieronymus** in ancient Greece. It then became **Geronimo** in Latin; and finally, Jerome. "Geronimo!" was the battle cry of World War II paratroopers as they jumped from their planes. It was not Latin they were yelling, but the name of a brave Apache Indian chief who refused to give up his fight. Nicknames for Jerome are Jer and Jerry.

Jesse (Hebrew). This is a boys' name from the Bible; it means "God's grace." The Biblical Jesse was the father of the great King David. Jake and Jess are nicknames. Jesse James was a famous bank robber and gunfighter who, with his brother Frank and other outlaws, formed the notorious James Gang. Jesse Owens was a famous Olympic track star who broke six world records in one day!

Jessica (Hebrew). Your pretty name is the feminine form of **Jesse,** and also means "God's grace." But here's a rewarding fact—your name also means "riches"! Nicknames are Jess, Jessie, and Jessy. Jessica Tandy and Jessica Lange are actresses.

Jill (Old English). How sweet it is—if your name is Jill! It means "a sweetheart." Jill was originally a short form for **Julia.** Then Jill became really popular on its own. Long ago, girls were often called "jills," and boys were often called "jacks." Another way to spell your name is **Gill.**

Joan, Joann, Joanna, Johanna (Hebrew). All these pretty names mean "God's gracious gift." Like **Jane** and others, they are feminine forms of **John**. A popular nickname for Joan is Joanie. Four film actresses are Joan Crawford, Joanne Woodward, Joan Fontaine, and Joan Collins. Long ago, a teenaged girl named Joan of Arc led the French army to victory. She is the patron saint of France.

Jocelyn (Latin). Jocelyn comes from the ancient Roman name **Justine** and means "just," "fair," and "honest." This pretty name also means "merry" and "joyous." **Joslyn** is the boys' version.

Jodie, Jody—see Judith.

Joel (Hebrew). Your name means "the Lord is God." The original Joel was a famous prophet in the Bible. Joel Grey is a singer-dancer-actor of stage and screen fame. Joel Chandler Harris was a writer of American folk tales called the Uncle Remus stories.

Joey—see Joseph.

John (Hebrew). If your name is John, you're really at the top—because John has been the most popular name in history! It means "God is gracious" or "God's gracious gift."

A popular name for John exists in almost every language. In Ireland it's **Sean** or **Shamus;** in Scotland, it's **Ian**. It's **Giovanni** or **Gianni** in Italy; **Juan** in Spain; **Jean** in France; **Jan** in Denmark; and **Johannes** or **Hans** in Germany and the Netherlands. In Russia the name is **Ivan.** Popular nicknames for John are Jack and Johnny. All told, eighty-four saints, twenty-three popes, four U.S. presidents, and countless kings have been named John. Other famous Johns are Little John (*Robin Hood*); Long John Silver (*Treasure Island*); and from the real world, record-breaking football great, Johnny Unitas; singers John Lennon and John Denver; and senator and former astronaut, John Glenn. Most famous John: John Doe, a name for Mr. Average Person in the U.S. of A.

Jonathan (Hebrew). Surprisingly, this name is not a variation of John, but a longer version of **Nathan,** which means simply "a gift." Jon is a neat nickname. In the Bible, Jonathan was King David's best friend.

Joseph (Hebrew). Your name means "He shall add" or "God shall add." The Bible says that when Joseph was born, Rachel, his mother, chose the name Joseph for him because it means "God shall add," and she wanted a second son. (She got him.) When Joseph grew up, he landed in Egypt, where his great wisdom saved both Egypt and his people from famine.

Joseph is **Giuseppe, Beppo,** or **Peppo** in Italy; **Jose, Pepe,** or **Pepito** in Spain; **Jozef** or **Jose** in Germany; and **Joseef** or **Oseep** in Russia. The feminine version of this name is **Josephine.** Joe, Jo, Jo-Jo, and Joey are popular nicknames, and a "good Joe" is a really nice guy.

Some famous Joes are baseball's "Joltin' Joe" DiMaggio, who slugged his way into the Hall of Fame, and former football star Joe Namath, who won a Super Bowl game for the New York Jets with his confidence and passing.

Joshua (Hebrew). Your name means "whom God has saved" or "the Lord saves." In the Bible, Joshua knocked down the walls of Jericho with sound waves! He had seven priests blow on rams' horns while all the people shouted their loudest! More recently, there was an inventor named Joshua, better known by his middle name, Lionel. Joshua Lionel Cowen invented the electric model train, which is sometimes called the Lionel train. A Joshua tree is a tall, cactuslike plant that grows in the desert.

Joy, Joyce (Old French, Latin). You can really feel lucky if you have either of these names! Both mean "to rejoice," "to delight," and "a jewel." Whether your name is Joy or Joyce, you're bound to bring good cheer wherever you go!

Juanita—see Jane.

Judith, Judy (Hebrew). Consider yourself "praised" if you are called Judith, for that is what your name means. It comes from **Judah,** and that name means "one who lives in Judea" (ancient Israel). **Judy,** a nickname for Judith, has become popular on its own, and so have **Judi** and **Judie.** The names **Jodie** and **Jody** are variations. Actress Judy Garland won a lasting place in movie stardom as Dorothy in *The Wizard of Oz* (1939). By the way, Judy's *real* name was Frances Gumm!

Julia, Julian, Julie, Jules, Juliet, Julius (Latin, Greek). All these names come from **Julius** and mean "belonging to the family or tribe of Julius." The best-known member is Julius Caesar, a great general during the days of the Romans. The Greek meanings are "the soft-haired or downy-bearded one"; or simply "a youth." **Gillian** is another form of this name. Julie is a popular name and a nickname for Julia and Juliet. **Julienne, Julietta,** and **Juliana** are other variations. Singer-actress Julie Andrews is a film and stage star. Julia Ward Howe wrote "The Battle Hymn of the Republic." Jules Verne was an early sci-fi writer who wrote *Journey to the Center of the Earth, 20,000 Leagues Under the Sea,* and other fantastic adventures.

June, Juneth (Latin). As everyone knows, June is a beautiful month and a time of great beginnings—summer, vacation, weddings. It's a happy month to be named for. And there's more—your name, and the month's name, both stem from the Roman goddess **Juno.** She was queen of the gods and the goddess of all women, so your name also means "queenly power"! Junie is a favorite nickname. June Cunningham Croly was one of the first female newspaper reporters in the U.S. She wrote her news stories under the pen name of Jennie June. June Allyson is a film actress.

Justin, Justine (Latin). Your name means "justice" or "honesty" because of the great Roman emperor, Justinian. He was well known for his fairness and wisdom, and was called "the Just." Two nicknames for Justin are Jos or Jus.

Karen (Greek, Danish). Your pretty name means "pure" and "purity." But did you know that your popular name is Danish? It is actually a shortened form of **Katherine.** Some other pretty ways to spell your name are: **Karin, Karyn, Caren,** and **Carina.** In France, your name is **Caron;** in Norway, **Karena** or **Karin.**

Karl, Karla—see Charles.

Katherine, Kathy (Greek). You can spell your famous name with a *C* or a *K*—take your pick. In ancient Greece it was Katherine, but when it became popular in olden England the English didn't have a *K* in their alphabet, so it became Catherine. However you spell it, your name means "pure." It's a popular name and turns up as **Katina** in Greece; **Katchen, Katrina,** or **Kathe** in Germany; **Katya** or **Katinka** in Russia; **Catalina** in Spain; and **Caterina** in Italy. **Kathleen,**

Cathleen, or **Cathlin** are Irish names and have meanings in addition to "pure"—they mean "beautiful-eyed," "star," and "beam of the waves." A host of interesting names and nicknames stem from Katherine. Some are: **Cathy, Kathie, Kate, Kathryn, Kathleen, Katie, Caitlin, Kit, Kitty, Cass, Cassie, Ina, Kara, Trina, Kay, Cat, Catie,** and **Katty.** Catherine the Great was an Empress of Russia. Many queens and saints have been named Catherine.

Kay (Greek). Originally a nickname for **Katherine,** this name now stands independently on its own. It means "pure," and it also means "to rejoice."

Keith (Irish, Scottish). If your name is Keith, you can choose from "wood," "wind," "a wood dweller," or "a place." Keith also means "swift as the wind," if you like to run. A long line of noble Scots earls once bore the name of Keith, and it has always been a popular name in Scotland. An unusual nickname is Kiki.

Kelly (Irish). Your name is a case of last things first! Kelly was originally a last name in Ireland and meant "a warrior." It then became a nickname for Irish actors and comedians. Now it's a first name and a pretty one, too! As you probably know, kelly green is a brilliant, bright, and beautiful shade of green.

Kenneth (Celtic). Your name means "chief" because of Kenneth, the first king of Scotland. Kenneth also means "a handsome leader." Kim, Kenn, Kennet, Kent, Ken, and Kenny are popular nicknames.

Kerstin—see Christina.

Kevin (Celtic). A truly nice name; it means "kind," "gentle," and "beloved." Kevin is a really popular name in Ireland and Scotland, as well as in this country. A favorite nickname is Kev.

Kimberly, Kim (Celtic). Your name means "the little valley or meadow." Kim, often a nickname for Kimberly, has become really popular on its own as a name for both boys and girls. It may have originally come from as far away as Korea. Kim Hunter, Kim Stanley, Kim Darby, and Kim Novak are all screen actresses. The Kimberly Diamond, named for the famous Kimberly diamond mine in South Africa, is one of the most valuable gems in the world.

Kirsten, Kristen—see Christina.

Kurt—see Conrad.

Kyle (Irish). Kyle started out as a boys' name, but has now become popular for girls. Kyle can mean "fair and handsome," "living near a chapel," or "a narrow channel."—take your pick! **Cuyler** and **Kyle** are two other forms of your name; **Kyla** was an early name for girls.

Lainie—see Elaine.

Lana—see Alan.

Laraine—see Lorraine.

Laura, Laurie, Lora, Loree, Lori (Latin). Your name means "the laurel or bay tree" and comes from the name **Laurence**. (See **Laurence** for more information.) Laurie is a favorite nickname for Laura, as well as a popular name on its own. Other forms of your name are **Laurinda, Lorna, Lorry, Loretta, Lauretta,** and **Laureen**. Laura Ingalls Wilder wrote about her pioneering childhood in the *Little House* books.

Laurel, Lauren (Latin). Like **Laura,** both Laurel and Lauren come from the name **Laurence** and mean "the laurel or bay tree." (See **Laurence** for more information.) Some variations of your name are **Loren, Lorin, Lorene,** and **Lorinda.** Beautiful Lauren Hutton is a well-known fashion model and movie star.

Laurence, Lawrence (Latin). Your distinguished name is a "place" name and it's also related to victory. Laurentium was an ancient city, the "city of laurels." Your name also means "the laurel or bay tree," whose evergreen leaves were woven into victory wreaths and used to crown the heroes and athletes in ancient Greece and Rome. This is where the expression "to win your laurels" comes from. **Larkin** and **Lorenzo** are other forms of Laurence. Nicknames are Larry and Laurie.

Leah, Lea, Lia (Hebrew). Your name means "the weary" or "the forsaken." In the Bible, Leah was Jacob's first wife and the mother of many sons. Lea, a nickname for Leah, has become a popular name, too. Lea may also stem from the name **Leo,** which gives it the extra meaning of "lioness." **Lee,** another nickname, is also popular independently.

Lee, Leigh (Old English). A good name for both boys and girls, Lee means "a meadow" or "sheltered." Lee is also a distinguished last name. Lee Grant is an actress of TV and movie fame; Lee Trevino is a champion golfer; Lee DeForest is the man who made it possible for you to hear the shows on TV today—he invented sound systems used first in radio and then in TV.

Lela, Leila, Lelah, Lelia—see Lillian.

Leonard (Latin, German). Your name is really grr-eat! It means "a lion" and "brave and strong as a lion," and is actually a longer version of the names **Leon** and **Leo**. (Leo means "lion" in Latin.) **Lennart** and **Lionel** are other forms of this name. In Italy and Spain, your name is spelled **Leonardo**. Lenny, Lennie, Len, and Leo are all popular nicknames. You may know Leonard Nimoy who plays the Vulcan, Mr. Spock, in *Star Trek* and narrates *In Search Of*—on TV. Leonardo da Vinci was a remarkable Italian artist who dreamed up modern engineering marvels about five hundred years ago.

Leonna, Lenore, Leonora, Lena—see Eleanor.

Leroy, Leroi (French). Hold your head up high if this is your name! It means "the king" and "royalty." Other versions of your name are **Elroy, Rex, Regis,** and just plain **King!** Roy is a favorite nickname. Former baseball great Leroy "Satchel" Paige became a living legend as the oldest person to pitch in a major league game—he was fifty-nine years old. Elroy Hirsch was a famous L.A. Rams football player known for catching a record seventeen touchdown passes in a single season. His nickname was "Crazy Legs."

Lesley, Leslie (Celtic, Scottish). Your name can mean "from the gray fort or stronghold" or "the low meadow." Long ago Leslie was the name of many Scottish noblemen. Leslie was once the name for boys and Lesley for girls, but it is now spelled either way for boys or girls.

Lester (English). This name comes from the English town of Leicester, which means "camp of the legion." It's also closely related to the name **Chester**. (See **Chester** for more information.) Another meaning for Lester is "the shining." A favorite nickname is Les.

Lewis, Louis, Ludwig, Luis (German). Your name means "famous warrior" and "famous in battle." The early German version of this name was **Hludwig**! It then became Ludwig, and finally Louis. Other forms of your name are **Lewes, Lewie, Lew,** or even **Aloysius** (Al-oh-wish-us). There have been many kings of France named Louis, and many kings of Germany were named Ludwig. Popular nicknames are Lou, Louie, and Looey. Lou Gehrig, known as the "Iron Man," was one of the greatest baseball players of all time.

Lidia—see Lydia.

Lillian, Lily (Latin). Your name means "a lily" and is one of the oldest of the "flower names." The lovely, fragrant, white Easter lily is the symbol of life, renewal, and purity, and there are many exotic lilies, too. The name Lily is a shortened version of Lillian. Other variations are: **Lilly, Lela, Leila, Lelah, Lelia, Lila, Lilia, Lilian, Lilyan, Lilas, Lillis,** and **Liliona**. Favorite nicknames are Lil, Lillie, and Lilli.

Linda (Spanish). Your popular name means "pretty or beautiful," and originally came from longer names like **Melinda, Rosalinda,** or **Belinda. Lynda** is another way to spell your name. Nicknames are Lin, Lynd, Lind, Lyn, and **Lynn**, which is a name in its own right.

Lindsay, **Lindsey** (German). This name is popular for both boys and girls and means "from the linden tree by the sea." In England, your name might be spelled **Linsey** or **Lyndsey.** A nickname is Lin.

Lindy—see Melinda.

Linn—see Lynn.

Lionel—see Leonard.

Lisa (Hebrew). Your name is definitely one of the popular names today! It means "oath of God," "dedicated to God," or "house of joy." Lisa probably comes from **Elizabeth.** (See **Elizabeth** for more information.) One of the world's most famous paintings bears your name: the slightly smiling *Mona Lisa,* by Leonardo da Vinci. The model's name was Lisa del Gioconda. This beautiful painting has been valued at $100 million dollars!

Liza, Lisbeth, Lisabet—see Elizabeth.

Lois (Greek). You are "the better one" if this is your name, for you are "pleasing" and "desirable" to have around. Lois is sometimes a boys' name and is sometimes spelled **Loyce.**

Lola—see Dolores.

Loren—see Laurel.

Lorna, Loretta—see Laura.

Lorraine (French). Your pretty name means "a girl from Lorraine," a beautiful region of France. Some say however, that Lorraine originally came from **Louis,** which would give your name a different meaning: "famous warrior." Other ways to spell your name are **Loraine** and **Laraine.**

Louisa, Louise (German). Both pretty names are feminine forms of **Louis** and mean "a famous warrior" and "famous in battle." Long ago, your name was spelled **Heloise.** Other forms are **Eloise, Allison, Allie, Lois, Luette,** and **Lulu.** In France, it's **Aloyse** or **Lisette**; in Italy, **Eloisa** or **Luisa**; in Spain, it's **Luisa,** too; in Germany, it's **Luise.** A nice nickname is Lou. Louisa May Alcott wrote a story based on her family called *Little Women.*

Lucas—see Luke.

Lucille, Lucy (Latin). You can brighten up anybody's life if this is your name, because it means "light"! A Roman goddess of the moon was Lucina. Lucy, a nickname for Lucille, has also become popular as a first name. Other variations of your name are **Lucia, Lucie, Lucinda, Lucilla, Lucile, Lucette,** and **Lulu; Lucien** is the masculine form. Lucille Ball's funny antics as Lucy have been making TV audiences laugh for over thirty years!

Luke (Latin). Luke means "light," and originally came from the Roman name, **Lucius.** It then became **Lucien,** then finally Luke. Other forms of your name are **Lucas** and **Lucifer,** which means "the light bringer." (Early matches were called "lucifers.")

Lydia, Lidia (Greek). Your dignified name was once the name of a famous city. Lydia was known for its wealthy citizens, its beautiful women, and its culture. So your name, which means "from Lydia," also means "beauty, wealth, and culture." Liddy is a nickname.

Lynda—see Linda.

Lynn, Linn, Lynne (Irish). "A waterfall" or "a pool" are the meanings of your popular name. Lynn and Lynne originally came from longer names like **Lynnet** and **Lynette.** Lyn and Lynnie are popular nicknames.

Marc—see Mark.

Marcia, Marcie, Marcy, Marsha (Latin). These gentle names all come from Mars, the Roman god of war, and mean "a warrior." A windy month and a planet are also named for Mars. Marcia used to be a favorite name for girls born in March. **Marcella** and **Marcelle** are other forms of your name.

Margaret (Latin, Greek). Your name means "pearl" and also "a child of moonlight." All these names come from Margaret: **Margery, Margie, Marjorie, Marge, Meg, Madge, Maggie, Maisie, Peg, Peggy,** and **Rita.** Some are nicknames for Margaret; all have become popular first names. Some foreign spellings are popular here, too: **Marguerite** or **Margot** from France; **Greta** or **Gretchen** from Germany; and **Megan** from Ireland.

Margery—see Marjorie.

Maria, Marie (Hebrew, Latin). Both names mean "bitterness," the same as their source, **Mary.** Maria is a Latin name; Marie is French. A nickname for Marie is Mimi. In 1893, Marie Owen became the first female police officer in America. Marie Curie, a famous French scientist, discovered radium and is the only person to have won two Nobel Prizes. Marie Mitchell was a famous astronomer. (See **Mary** for more information.)

Marian, Marion, Marianne, Mary Ann. All these variations of **Mary** stem from the Italian name, **Mariana.** They all mean "of bitter grace," since Mariana is a combination of Mary ("bitter") and Ann ("grace"). **Marianne** is the French version. In the classic story *Robin Hood,* Maid Marion is Robin Hood's true love.

Marilyn (Hebrew). If your name is Marilyn it all adds up; just add Mary and Lynn. Since Mary means "bitter" and Lynn means "a waterfall" or "a pool," Marilyn, naturally enough, means "a bitter waterfall or pool." Another possible meaning is "bitter tears." A neat nickname is Lyn.

Marjorie, Margery, Marjory (Scottish). Your name is a popular one in Scotland, as well as in this country. It's a version of Margaret and can mean either "a pearl" or "a child of moonlight." (See **Margaret** for more information.) Nicknames are Marjie, Margie, and Marge.

Mark (Latin). Mark down this fact: Your name is one of the most popular around! Like the month March and the girls' name **Marcia,** Mark comes from Mars, the Roman god of war, and means "of Mars" and "a warrior." **Marc, Marco,** and **Marcel** are other forms of Mark. Swimmer Mark Spitz has won the greatest number of Olympic gold medals: seven. Mark Twain (real name: Samuel Clemens) wrote *The Adventures of Tom Sawyer.* Italian explorer Marco Polo traveled to China and brought spaghetti home to Italy!

Martha (Aramaic—a language of ancient Israel). Martha means "mistress of the house" and "a lady." It used to be that a good housewife was sometimes called "a Martha." Your name comes from the Biblical Martha, who was famous for her excellent housekeeping and fine hospitality. In fact, Saint Martha is the patron saint of housewives. **Marta** is another version of your name, and Marty and Mattie are popular nicknames. The most famous Martha is probably Martha Washington; she was this country's *first* First Lady.

Martin, Martina, Martine (Latin). All three names come from Mars, the Roman god of war, and mean "a warrior." Mart, Marty, or Martie are popular nicknames. The "Red Fox" was a nickname for our eighth president, Martin Van Buren. Martin Luther King fought peacefully in the 1960s for civil rights. Martina Navratilova is a champion tennis star.

Marvin (German). "Famous friend" or "sea friend" are the meanings of this name, which is also a relative of the name **Irving**. Other versions of Marvin are **Merwin** and **Mervin;** Marv is a popular nickname. Marvin is often a last name as well as first name.

Mary (Hebrew). Mary is one of the most frequently given names of all time! Many saints and queens have had this name, and it's always been a favorite in songs and stories. Mary comes from the Hebrew *mara* or *marah*, a place of bitter waters. In Greek and Latin, Mary sometimes meant "star of the sea" or "lady of the sea." Many names come from Mary: **Marie, Marion, Maria, Marla, Marya, Molly, Polly, Minnie, May, Mamie, Maureen, Mariot, Mariam, Moira,** and **Maura.** Mary also teams up nicely with other names: **Mary Ann, Mary Lou, Mary Ellen, Mary Jane,** and **Mary Jo** are just a few. The book *Frankenstein,* on which the movie was based, was written by Mary Shelley.

Mary Ann—see Marian.

Matthew (Hebrew). The original spelling of your name—**Mattathias**—was a mouthful, but the meaning of your name is much easier to swallow: It's "a gift of the Lord." Popular nicknames are Matt, Matty, and Mattie. Matthew Brady was the first really well known photographer; his remarkable pictures of the Civil War are considered classics today.

Maureen (Irish). Your name comes from Mary and means "bitter." It's a really popular name in Ireland where it also has another meaning—"the dark one." **Maura** and **Maurine** are two other versions of your name. A popular nickname is Mo. Two beautiful movie stars were Maureen O'Sullivan and Maureen O'Hara.

May—see Mary.

Meg, Megan—see Margaret.

Melanie (Greek). "The dark" or "black" is the meaning of your pretty name, because of **Melania,** or Demeter, the Greek goddess of the earth. She would sadly wear black clothing all winter until her daughter, Persephone, returned in the spring from the underworld to visit her. Melanie also means "very kind," like Melanie in the film *Gone With the Wind*. Favorite nicknames are Mel, Mellie, and Melly.

Melinda, Malinda (Greek). Yours is a really nice name, and it has a nice meaning, too! It means "gentle." Some name experts think that since the name **Linda** might have originally come from Melinda, your name, like Linda, may also mean "beautiful or pretty." **Lindy** is a neat nickname and also a name on its own.

Melissa (Greek). Your name means "honey" or "honey-sweet," and was originally spelled **Melitus.** In Greek myth, a pretty wood nymph named Melissa first taught men how to use good-tasting honey. Altogether, your name adds up to "pleasant and good." Some names that come from Melissa are **Millicent, Millie, Lissa, Lisse,** and **Melita. Melisse** and **Melisande** are French names; **Melisenda** is Spanish. Nicknames are Missy, Mel, Mellie, and Lissa.

Melvin, Melvyn (Celtic). This name means "a leader or chieftain." Mel is a favorite nickname. Melvyn Douglas was a popular Hollywood actor of the '30s and '40s, whose distinguished film career spanned over fifty years.

Meredith (Welsh). Once pretty much a last name, Meredith has become popular as a first name for both boys and girls. Its meaning is "protector of the sea" or "great chief." Merry is a cheery nickname.

Mervin—see Marvin.

Meryl, Merle, Muriel (Arabic). All these names come from the word *myrrh,* a precious but bitter-tasting ointment. Myrrh was used in ancient times for making perfume and incense and for healing certain kinds of wounds. It was also one of the three gifts that the Wise Men gave the baby Jesus. Merle has a meaning of its own; it is the French word for "blackbird."

Michael (Hebrew). Michael is definitely one of the most popular names! It began with the Bible, where the archangel Michael was called "the Prince of Angels" and one "who is like unto the Lord." This last is the true meaning of the name, so consider yourself blessed! Names that have come from Michael are: **Mitchell, Mitch,** and **Mickey** (boys), and **Michaela, Michelle,** and **Michele** (girls). In France, Michael is **Michel;** in Spain, **Miguel;** in Russia, **Mikhail** or **Misha.** Favorite nicknames are Mike, Mickey, and Mick. Famous Michaels: actors Michael Landon and Mickey Rooney; and former Yankee great Mickey Mantle, truly one of baseball's all-time stars.

Michele, Michelle (Hebrew). This pretty name is the feminine form of Michael and means "who is like unto the Lord." **Michal** was the original, Biblical spelling. Yours is a really popular name in France. Neat nicknames are Midge and Micki.

Mickey—see Michael.

71

Mildred, Millie (Anglo-Saxon). "Mild," "strength," and "mild strength" are the meanings of this name. The first known Mildred was a princess of ancient Britain who was called **Mildthryth.** Millie, a favorite nickname, has also become popular independently.

Millicent—see Melissa.

Milton (Old English). Your name means "by the mill town or farm" or "from the mill farmstead." Milt and Miltie are popular nicknames. Comedian Milton Berle was a favorite TV star of the 1950s. He is still known as "Uncle Miltie" and "Mr. Television."

Mindy (German). Your name means "loving memory" or "sweet remembrance." Mindy was originally a nickname from **Minna** or **Wilhelmina,** but it really stands on its own now as an independent name. Another version of this name is **Minda.**

Miriam (Hebrew). This ancient Bible name may be related to Mary or *marrah*, which means bitterness, but Miriam has some additional meanings—"sorrow," "sea of bitterness," and even earlier, "mistress of the sea." In the Bible, Miriam was a prophetess and the sister of Aaron. She led a song of triumph as the Israelites passed through the Red Sea.

Mitchell—see Michael.

Molly, Mollie (Hebrew). Your name was once a nickname for either **Mary** or **Miriam.** Nowadays it's almost always used independently. During the Revolutionary War, Molly Pitcher carried water for thirsty soldiers; she heroically took over for her husband, a cannoneer, after he collapsed. Molly's real name was Mary Ludwig Hays McCauley. (See **Mary** for more information.)

Monica (Latin). If your name is Monica, you probably give good advice; anyway, your name means "an adviser" or "I advise." Monica probably came from the name **Dominica,** which means "the Lord's Day" or "Sunday." Girls born on Sunday are often given this name. In France, your name is **Monique** or **Dominique.**

Muriel—see Meryl.

N

Nancy (Hebrew). Your name means "grace" or "graciousness." Once a nickname for **Ann** or **Hannah,** Nancy has become a popular name on its own. Nan and Nanny are nicknames for Nancy, and **Nan** is sometimes a regular first name. The French have a seaport called Nancy, but their girls' name is **Nanette.** Topping the list of favorite Nancys is super-sleuth Nancy Drew, popular with readers since 1930. Nancy Reagan is the wife of our fortieth president, Ronald Reagan.

Naomi (Hebrew). "Beautiful, pleasant, and sweet" are the meanings of this truly nice name. You can get a happy new meaning of your name, however, if you just switch two letters. Then it becomes the Arabic name **Noami,** which means "felicity" (happiness).

Natalie (Latin). Many happy returns should be yours if Natalie is your name—it means "natal day" or "birthday"! Natalie has other meanings: "child of Christmas" and "birthday of the Lord." It is almost as popular as the name Carol for girls born around Christmastime. Natalie in French is **Noel** or **Noelle;** in Russia, it's **Natalia, Natalya,** or **Natasha.** Nat or Netty are nicknames.

Nathan, Nathon, Nathaniel (Hebrew). These names are almost the same but not quite! Nathan means "a gift," but Nathaniel has a slightly longer meaning— " a gift of God." It was once spelled **Nathanael.** Some neat nicknames are Nat, Natty, Nate, and Than. Schoolteacher Nathan Hale got caught when he spied for the patriots in the American Revolution; Nat King Cole was the king of pop singers in the '50s.

Ned —see Edward.

Neil (Irish). Originally the name of many Irish heroes and kings, Neil means "courageous," "the champion," or "the chief." Other versions of your name are **Neal, Neill, Niel, Nial, Nealey,** and **Nealon.** A courageous astronaut, Neil Armstrong, was the first man to walk on the moon.

Nena — see Nina.

Nicholas (Greek). This name means "victory of the people." Other forms of your name are **Nicol, Nichol,** and **Nicolas.** Popular nicknames are Nick and Nicky. The best-known Nicholas is St. Nicholas, or St. Nick, whom we know as Santa Claus.

Nicole (Greek). This name has always been popular in France, but it's gaining popularity in this country, too. Nicole comes from **Nicholas,** and its meaning is the same—"victory of the people." Another way to spell it is **Nicol. Nicolette** and **Colette** are two other French versions. (Colette also means "a necklace.") In Italy, the name is **Nicola;** in Greece, **Nicolina.** Neat nicknames are Nikki and Colie.

Nina. Your name probably came from **Nanine,** a French form of **Ann,** meaning "grace." But Nina may also mean "granddaughter" or "great-granddaughter" (Hebrew), or "a little girl" (Spanish)— the choice is yours! Some Ninas like to pronounce their name "nee-nah"; others prefer "nine-ah." **Ninetta** and **Nena** are other versions of this name. A popular nickname is Nin. A very famous Nina was one of Christopher Columbus's three ships—a ship is always a "she"!

Noah (Hebrew). Sit down, kick off your sneakers, and take it easy because your name means "rest and relaxation," "peace and quiet," and "comfort." Your name comes from the Bible, of course, where you will find the famous story of Noah and the Ark.

Noel, Noelle (French, Latin). Like Carol, Noel is both a boys' and a girls' name. It means "song of joy" and is the French word for Christmas. Noel also means "a child of Christmas," so it is a perfect name for children born at Yuletide.

Nora — see Eleanor.

Norma (Latin). Norma is probably a form of **Norman,** but it has another meaning, too. It means "the model or pattern, or example."

Norman (Scandinavian). If you are a Norman, you have many possible meanings to choose from because the Normans have always been doers. The name means "Northman" or "man from the north." But there's more. How about "seafarer," "raider," or "conqueror"? Long ago, fierce Vikings from Norway raided the French and English coasts.

Finally, these Normans in northern France invaded England under William the Conqueror in 1066. The Norman knights brought a rich culture to England. A famous Norman king was Richard I, "the Lionhearted." Norm and Normie are nicknames for Norman.

O

Oliver, Olivia, Olive (Latin). In ancient times, the olive branch was a symbol of peace, and your name came to mean "a man or woman of peace" or "peaceful." **Olaf,** the Norwegian version of Oliver, is a popular name in Norway. Neat nicknames are Liv, Livy, Ollie, Olly, Nolly, and Noll. Comedian Oliver Hardy was the larger half of the comedy team of Laurel and Hardy. Actress Olivia de Havilland played romantic heroines in the movies. Beautiful Olivia Newton-John is one of today's most popular female singers.

Oscar (German, Celtic). There are two possible meanings for this name: "divine spear" (German) or "leaping warrior" (Celtic). Oscar has been the name of many kings of Norway and Sweden. **Oskar** is another version; Osc is a nickname. Hollywood Academy Award winners receive a little gold statuette called an "Oscar."

Otto (German). This name was a favorite with ancient emperors of Germany and means "wealthy and prosperous." It's also a palindrome—spelled the same way both backward and forward.

Owen (Latin, Welsh). Owen comes from the name **Evan** and means "a youth" or "a young warrior." An earlier spelling of Owen is **Ywain.** Sir Ywain was one of the most famous knights of King Arthur's legendary Round Table. Owen rates as the most popular name in the country of Wales. Other forms of your name are **Bowen** and **Ewan.** All these names are also last names.

P

Page, **Paige** (Greek). Long ago, pages were young men who trained to become knights. Since then, Page has become a popular girls' name. Its meanings is "a child" or "young." Page is frequently a last name, too.

Pamela (Greek, English). Your name means either "all honey" or "honey elf." Either way, it's a sweet name; but the "all honey" meaning just may have been invented! Some say that the writer, Sir Philip Sydney, combined the Greek words *pan* (all) and *meli* (honey) to create Pamela. The name Pamela was later launched in a novel called *Pamela* by Richardson.

Patricia, **Patrice** (Latin). Your name means "of noble birth," "nobility," and "noble woman." The patricians were the wealthy and noble citizens of ancient Rome. **Pat, Patty, Patti, Patsy, Tish, Tricia, Trish,** and **Trixie** are all nicknames for Patricia.

Patrick (Latin). Your name, like **Patricia,** means "of noble birth," "nobility," and also "a nobleman." Patrick is the most popular name in Ireland because of Saint Patrick, who, legend has it, rid that country of snakes. Today, St. Patrick's Day is joyfully celebrated here and in Ireland. Nicknames are Pat, Patsy, Paddy, Ricky, and Rick. Patrick Henry, an early American statesman, said, "Give me liberty or give me death!"

Paul (Latin). Although "small" and "little" are the meanings of this name, it is a popular name in every country. The Paulians were a famous family in ancient Rome, and the name comes from them. Famous Pauls: Paul Revere, the night rider who alerted American patriots that "the British are coming"; Paul McCartney, singer-songwriter, and a former Beatle. Now he has his own group, Wings.

Paula, **Pauline** (Latin). This feminine version of **Paul** means the same thing—"small" or "little." In France, it's **Paulette** or **Pauline.** In Russia, Paula is **Pavla.** Polly is a nickname.

Pearl (Latin). This lovely "gem" name means "like a pearl." It also means "pear," because there are many pear-shaped pearls. The softly glowing jewel is found in oysters and, if perfect, is very valuable.

Peggy—see Margaret.

Penelope (Greek). Your name means "a weaver," "silent weaver," and also "faithful." In the Greek tales of Ulysses, Penelope, his faithful wife, waited seven years for her husband to return home from the Trojan Wars. Everyone said he was dead and suitors pressed her to marry them. Penelope said she would remarry when she finished the huge tapestry she was weaving. But every night she would unravel what she had woven during the day. Her faithfulness was finally rewarded. Ulysses did come home, after some really incredible adventures! **Penny** is a nickname for Penelope, and it has also become a popular name on its own. Pen and Pennie are nicknames, too.

Peter (Greek). Your name means "a rock" or "a stone" and comes from the Greek word for rock, *petra*. **Petros** is Peter in Greek. In Italy, it's **Pietro, Piero,** or **Petruccio;** in Spain, **Pedro;** in France, **Pierre** or **Pierrot.** Popular nicknames are Pete, Petie, and Petey. In the classic story, Peter Pan was the boy who never grew up.

Philip, **Phillip, Philippa, Pippa** (Greek). Don't hesitate to "get on your high horse" if any one of these names is yours, because they all mean "a lover of horses." Two other meanings are "a warrior" and "warlike." The original Philip was Philip of Macedonia, an ancient Greek warrior king who loved horses. Boys in France are called **Philippe;** in Spain, **Felipe.** Phil, Pip, and even Flip are some neat nicknames.

Phyllis (Greek). This pretty name has two meanings—"a green bough or branch" and "a little green leaf." The original Phyllis was a princess in the Greek myths who was turned into an almond tree. Other versions of this name are **Phillis** and **Phyllida.** Phyl and Phil are nicknames.

Polly (Hebrew). Polly is a really popular name on its own now. Once it was a nickname for **Mary** (and it still is for **Pauline**). Some think that Polly was made up to rhyme with Molly, another Mary nickname! Since Polly comes from Mary, one meaning must be "bitterness." Polly from Pauline would be "little." It also means "a young girl." A nice nickname is Poll. Polly and Anna were once teamed up together to make *Pollyanna,* a book by Eleanor Porter. Pollyanna always looked on the bright side of things and was such a "glad girl" that super-cheerful people are sometimes called "pollyannas."

Priscilla (Latin). Priscilla is one of many praised by Paul in the Bible. However, your name is Roman and means "the ancient," and it comes from the famous Priscus family. This ancient Roman family was known for the ability of its members to live to a very old age. Priscilla became a popular name in this country through the Pilgrim bride, Priscilla Alden. Popular nicknames are Pris, Prissie, Prissy, and Cilla.

83

Q - R

Quentin (Latin). This name means "the fifth one," and was often given in ancient Rome to the fifth son in a family. The names **Quincy** and **Quinn** are first cousins of Quentin.

Rachel, Rachael (Hebrew). This pretty name means "a little lamb." Lambs have always been a symbol of gentleness and innocence, and today people often say "gentle as a lamb." Rachel in the Bible was Jacob's wife and clever Joseph's mother. **Rochelle** is a French form of Rachel. Neat nicknames are Rae, Ray, and Raye.

Ralph, Randolph (Old English). If you lived long ago, your name might have been **Raedwulf!** This ancient form of your name belonged to a fierce warrior who used the wolf as his personal symbol. Because of this, your name means "wolf-counsel." In England, Ralph is often pronounced "rafe." **Rolf, Rudolf,** and **Rudolph** are German; **Raoul** is French. A favorite nickname is Ralphie. Two names that come from Randolph are **Randall** and **Rollo.** Popular nicknames are Rand and Randy.

Raymond (German). You're really "in the know" if Raymond is your name, because it means "a wise counselor." Raymond also means "mighty protector" and was once a popular name among knights in ancient Germany. A favorite nickname is Ray. Famous Rays are well-known singer Ray Charles and Ray Bradbury, who writes popular science-fiction tales.

Rebecca, Rebekah (Hebrew). Your name means "to bind," and this has always referred to the strong "bonds" of marriage. In fact, when two people plan to get married, they are sometimes said to be "tying the knot"! Popular nicknames are Beck, Becky, Beckie, Bekki, and Reba. A classic that features a heroine named Rebecca is *Rebecca of Sunnybrook Farm*.

Regina (Latin). "A queen" or "one who rules" are the meanings of this very regal name. A pretty nickname is **Gina,** which is also a popular first name. Other nicknames are Reggie and Gine. The name **Regan** comes from Regina and is given to both boys and girls.

Reginald (German). This name can mean "strong ruler," "a chieftain," or "wise power"—take your pick! **Reynold, Ronald,** and **Rinaldo** are other versions of this name, and favorite nicknames are Reg, Reggie, and Rex.

Reuben (Hebrew). In the Bible, Reuben was the firstborn son of Jacob. When he was born, his mother (Leah) exclaimed, "Behold—a son!" So Reuben now means "behold—a son!" Other versions of this name are **Rubin, Ruben,** and **Ruvane.**

Rhoda—see Rose.

Richard (German). Your name means "wealthy and powerful" and "powerful ruler." Richard is one of the most popular boys' names around and rates a long list of nicknames: Rich, Richie, Ritchie, Rick, Ricky, Rickie, Dick, Dicky, Dickie, and Dickon. King Richard I of England was known as "the Lionhearted" because of his bravery and generous nature.

Rita—see Margaret.

Robert (German). In the name game, Robert is a double winner! It means "bright fame," and it is also fabulously popular. **Roberta** is the feminine version. Nicknames are Bob, Bobby, Rob, Robbie, Robin, and Bert. Famous Roberts include movie actor Robert Redford; Robert E. Lee, the Civil War general; and Rob Roy, a legendary Scottish outlaw.

Robin (German). Your name comes from **Robert** and also means "bright fame." Robin began as a boys' name, and it still is, but it has also become very popular for girls. Robin Hood was that very famous legendary outlaw who, with his band of merry men, stole from the rich and gave to the poor. When the robin redbreast appears, it's a sure sign that spring is here!

Rochelle—see Rachel.

Rodney (German) Your name means "famous" or "renowned." But it may also have originally come from a place in England called Rodney Stoke, which meant "an island of reeds." Popular nicknames are Rod and Roddy. Famous Rods: Former child actor, Roddy McDowell, who won fame as an adult starring in the *Planet of the Apes* movies, and longtime baseball batting champ, slugger Rod Carew.

Roger, Rodger (German). Your name means "famous spear" and, long ago, was a name given to great heroes of battle. During World War II, the word "roger" was used to mean "everything's all right" or "okay." A favorite nickname is Roge. Track star Roger Bannister was the first man ever to run the mile in under four minutes. New York Yankee home-run champ Roger Maris hit more home runs in a single season than any other player in baseball history.

Ronald (Scottish). Believe it or not, Ronald is actually a shortened version of the German name, **Reginald.** Ronald became popular in Scotland, and it means "a strong and mighty ruler." The feminine version is **Rona.** Ron and Ronnie are popular nicknames. Former actor Ronald Reagan is our fortieth president.

Rose (Latin). It's one of many "flower" names and means "a rose," of course! Whether they're pink, red, or yellow, or a color in between, roses are among the most prized flowers. A wide variety of names have come from Rose, such as **Rosalind** ("fair rose"), **Roseann** ("gracious rose"), **Rosa, Rosalie, Rosalyn, Rosemarie, Rosemary, Rosamond,** and **Rhoda.** Two pretty nicknames are Rosie and Rosy. A popular nickname for Rosalyn and Rosalind is Roz.

Rosemary (Latin). Your pretty name was originally **Mary Rose,** which meant "Mary's rose." Later, the names were switched to make Rosemary. The Rose and Mary meanings apply, of course (see **Rose** and **Mary** for more information), but your name also comes from the rosemary herb plant. Rosemary is said to grow best near the sea, and so your name also means "rose of the sea." Today this herb is used in flavoring, but long ago, rosemary was also used as a medicine—it was thought to be able to refresh the memory. Lucky you—you're both rosy and refreshing! Nicknames are Rose, Mary, Rosie, and Rosy.

Rowena (Celtic). A famous Rowena of ancient times was a legendary Saxon princess. She was called White Mane. Two other meanings of this pretty name are "flowering white hair" and "slender fair." The name probably became popular because of the fair Rowena, an Anglo-Saxon heroine in the classic story of knighthood, *Ivanhoe,* by Sir Walter Scott. Ro is a nickname.

Roxanne—see Dawn.

Roy (Latin). "The king" or "kingly" are the meanings of this name which, some name sources say, is really a shortened form of the name **Royal.** Others think that the name Roy may have originally come from an Irish word meaning "red." One of the greatest sports goofs of all time was made by a football player named Roy Reigels. In the 1929 Rose Bowl, this defensive lineman for USC blew the whole game by carrying the ball seventy yards in the wrong direction—to make a touchdown for the other team!

Ruben, Rubin—see Reuben.

Rudolf, Rudolph—see Ralph.

Russell (Old French). Your name means "redheaded" or "rusty-haired," and "like a fox." Long ago, in England, "russel" was another name for the red fox. Favorite nicknames are Rusty, Red, and, of course, Russ.

Ruth (Hebrew). Your pretty name means "beautiful friend," "friendship," or "a companion." The tale of Ruth and Naomi and their strong friendship is one of the most famous stories in the Bible. But because this same Ruth had such a hard life, the name has also come to mean "sorrowful." **Ruthia** and **Rue** are other versions of your name. Ruthie is a popular nickname. Most people think that the candy bar Baby Ruth was named after baseball great Babe Ruth—but it was actually named for one of President Grover Cleveland's daughters!

S

Sally—see Sara.

Samantha (Aramaic—a language of ancient Israel). In recent years, this pretty name has grown in popularity. Facts about its origins are few, however—but it does mean "a listener" and probably came from ancient Israel. Favorite nickname is Sam.

Samuel (Hebrew). Your name means "God has heard" or "name of God" because of Samuel in the Bible. Samuel was favored by the Lord and considered so wise by the people that the name Samuel came to mean "honored judge." Neat nicknames are Sam, Sammy, and Sammie. Famous Samuels include Samuel Morse, inventor of the Morse code and the telegraph; and Uncle Sam, the tall, white-bearded symbol of our country. His name came from the letters USAM, meaning the United States of America!

Sandra—see Alexandra.

ara, Sarah (Hebrew). Your name comes from the Bible and means "the princess." Sal and Sallie are nicknames. **Sally,** once a nickname for Sarah, has become popular as an independent name. Other names that have come from Sarah are **Sadye, Sadie,** and **Sarena.** Actress Sarah Bernhardt lived some time ago, but she was a fabulous performer in her day. *Sara Crewe* is a marvelous girls' story by Frances Hodgson Burnett.

cott (Scottish). Your name comes from Scotland and means "a Scot" or "a Scotsman." It also means "wanderer" since the original dwellers in ancient Scotland were wandering tribes. Popular nicknames are Scotty and Scottie. *Star Trek* fans will never forget Scottie, the sensible engineer on the Starship *Enterprise.* One of this country's earliest astronauts was Lieutenant Commander Scott Carpenter.

ean, Shawn (Irish). It's the Irish form of **John** and means "God is gracious." Some variations of your name are **Seamus, Shane, Shamus,** and **Shaun.** Shawn is a popular name for both boys and girls. (See **John** for more information.)

eymour. You can take your pick from three possible meanings: "the Moorish saint" (French-Latin); "famed at sea" (German); or "tailor" (Old English). Favorite nicknames are Sy, Si, and Cy. Seymour is frequently a last name.

haron (Hebrew). The "rose of Sharon" is a tall, flowering shrub that bloomed in ancient Israel—it was named for the land or village of Sharon. Your pretty name means "of the land of Sharon." **Shara** and **Shari** are neat nicknames, but they're also popular on their own.

heila, Sheilah (Irish). Your name is the Irish version of **Cecilia,** which means "the dim-sighted." However, Sheila has a melodic meaning all its own—it means "musical." Your lilting name is most popular in Ireland and is spelled in a variety of ways: **Sheilah, Sheelah, Shelagh,** or **Sheelagh.** One nickname for Sheila is simply, She.

heldon, Shelley (Old English). This is a "place" name which means "from a hill ledge," "a shelly meadow," or "a shield town." Shel is a favorite nickname for Sheldon. Another nickname, Shelley, has also become popular independently as a name for both boys and girls. Some say that the name Shelley honors Percy Bysshe Shelley, the great poet.

herry, Sheri, Sheree (Spanish or French). Your name comes from Jerez ("heh-rez"), a town in southern Spain that's famous for making a kind of wine called sherry. *Jerez* is actually the Spanish word for "sherry." Sheri may have also come from the French name, **Cherie,** which means "the dear one." **Sherile** is a variation.

Sheryl—see Cheryl.

hirley (English). Did you know that Shirley was once only a boys' name? It first became a popular girls' name during the 1800s when writer Charlotte Brontë gave the name to a heroine in one of her books. It's been a popular name for girls ever since and means "bright meadow" or "white meadow." The name may have originally come from a place in England called Shirley. Other ways to spell your name are **Shirly, Shirlee,** and **Shirlie.** Shirl and Shir are neat nicknames. Child actress Shirley Temple is still seen on TV in reruns of movies; *Heidi,* and *The Little Colonel,* were just a few. Shirley Jones and Shirley Maclaine are two modern day movie stars.

ibyl, Sybil (Greek). "Wise or prophetic" or "a prophetess" are the meanings of this name. In ancient Greece and Rome, the sibils were wise women who supposedly could foretell the future. Two pretty versions of this name are **Sibylla** and **Sybilla.** Sib and Sibbie are nicknames.

idney, Sydney (French). Your name means "a follower of Saint Denis." It came about by running the two words in the name Saint Denis (or Saint Denys) together and making a contraction. Girls are sometimes given this name, too. Nicknames are Sid and Syd.

imon, Simone (Hebrew). Your name means "he who hears" or "to be heard" and comes from the Bible, where it was first spelled **Simeon.** Simeon can also mean "a hyena"! Simone is popular in France. Nicknames are Si, Sim, or Simie. An ever-popular game is Simon Says. Simon Bolivar was a famous soldier and hero of South America. He is greatly honored in the country of Bolivia, which was named after him.

Sonia, Sonya—see Sophie.

ophie, Sophia (Greek). Your name means "wisdom" or "the wise one." Once Sophie was a nickname for Sophia, but nowadays it's become much more popular on its own. Two other relatives of this name are **Sonia** and **Sonya;** both are favorite names in eastern Europe and Russia. **Sophy** is another way to spell your name.

tacey, Stacy (Greek). Your name is shared by both boys and girls and was originally a nickname for either **Anastasia** or **Eustacia** (girls) or **Eustace** (boys). Anastasia means "immortal" or "the resurrection," while two meanings of Eustace and Eustacia are "steadfast" and "peaceful." Anastasia was a name often given to girls born around Easter time. One version of your name is **Stacia;** another way to spell it is **Stacie.**

tanley (English). This name means "a stony field" and comes from a place in England called Stoneleah. Neat nicknames are Stan and Stannie. Former baseball great Stan Musial was known as "Stan the Man."

Stella—see Esther.

tephanie (Greek). Yours is the feminine form of the name **Stephen** and means "a crown" or "a garland." (See **Stephen** for more information.) Other ways to spell it are **Stephana, Stefanie, Stephania,** and **Stephenie.** Popular nicknames are Steffi and Stephie.

Stephen, Steven (Greek). This is one of the most popular names around. It means "a crown" or "a garland" and comes from ancient Greece. It was originally the word for the crown or wreath that was awarded to athletic champions or heroes. In fact, your name was originally spelled **Stephanos,** which means "a champion." In France, it's **Etienne;** in Italy, **Stefano;** in Spain, **Esteban;** in Russia, **Stefon** and **Stepka.** Nicknames are Steve and Stevie.

Stewart, Stuart (English). Yours is a "job" name and means "a steward." A steward was someone hired to manage the large property and the household affairs of wealthy landowners. He would keep track of the servants, gardeners, and gamekeepers, collect rents from anyone who lived on the estate, and generally make sure that things were running smoothly. In fact, two other meanings for your name are "a caretaker" and "a keeper of an estate." Neat nicknames are Stu and Stewie.

Susan (Hebrew). This pretty name comes from the word *shushannah,* which means "a lily." Susan was originally spelled either **Susanna** or **Susannah,** and these versions are also seen today. **Suzan** is another way to spell it. In France, your name is **Suzanne, Susetta,** or **Suzette,** which means "little Susan"; in Italy and Spain, it's **Susanna;** in Germany, it's **Susanne.** Popular nicknames are Sue, Susie, Susy, and Suzie. An old-fashioned nickname for Susan was Sukey.

The name Susan has won fame in many different

ways—there's a flower called a black-eyed Susan, which is a yellow daisy; a lazy Susan, which is a revolving tray; a sweet Susan, a kind of plant with a pink-to-purple flower. Susan B. Anthony fought for women's rights in the 1800s; and the first woman mayor was Susanna Salter—she was the mayor of Argonia, Kansas in 1887.

Sybil—see Sibyl.

ylvia, Silvia (Latin). Since the word sylvan means "a wood," your pretty name means a "wood-dweller" or "a forest maiden." It was originally a name used by the ancient Romans to describe "a girl of the forest." **Sylvester** and **Silas** are the masculine versions. In France, your name is **Silvie.** Nicknames are Syl or Sil.

T

Tamara, Tammy, Tammie (Hebrew). Tammy has become a popular name on its own, but it's really a nickname for Tamara, which means "a palm tree." Tamara is a popular name in Russia because it was once the name of a legendary Russian princess. Your name comes from the Bible, where it was originally spelled **Tamar.** Tamar was the daughter of the great King David.

Terence, Terrence, Terry (Latin). This nice name means "soft and sweet" and "tender." The Terentian family was one of the most noble families in ancient Rome. Other forms of your name are **Torrance** and **Torey.** Terry is a nickname that is sometimes used as a name on its own. Both Terrence and Terry are really popular in Ireland. Terry in Irish means "the tower."

Theodore (Greek). Your name means "a gift of God" or "a divine gift." Sister names include **Dorothy, Dorothea,** and **Theodora.** A number of nicknames come from Theodore: Ted, Teddy, Tad, Thad, Ned, Neddy, Noddy, and Theo. Our twenty-sixth president, Theodore "Teddy" Roosevelt, was known as a great soldier and a man who liked to hunt. But on one of his hunting expeditions, he refused to shoot a helpless bear cub. Because of this, toymakers started making toy bears that they sold as "teddy bears," named after him. Teddy bears have been popular ever since!

Theresa, Terry (Greek). There are two meanings for this pretty name. It may mean "a reaper or harvester," or it may also mean "a girl from Therasia." (The Therasias are islands off the coast of Greece.) Another way to spell your name is **Treasa. Terry, Tracey, Tess, Tessie,** and **Tessa** are nicknames that have also become very popular as independent names. Terry has practically topped Theresa in popularity, and Tracey is slowly catching up! If you lived in Italy, you might be called **Teresa, Teresina,** or **Tersa;** in Spain, **Teresita;** in France, **Thérèse.**

Thomas (Hebrew). You might be seeing double if your name is Thomas because it means "a twin"! Thomas was a very popular name in Old England, and it's still a great favorite today. Thomas Jefferson, who wrote the Declaration of Independence, was one of this country's greatest statesmen. Tom Seaver is truly one of baseball's greatest pitchers. His nickname is "Tom Terrific." Thomas Alva Edison, a brilliant scientist, is best known for inventing the light bulb.

Timothy (Greek). Your name means "honoring and fearing God." An ancient way to spell it was **Timotheus.** Favorite nicknames are Tim and Timmy.

Toby, Tobey, Tobias (Hebrew, German). Your name can either mean "goodness of the Lord" or "a dove." Toby is actually a nickname for the name Tobias, but it's become popular as a name on its own. Both boys and girls are named Toby.

Todd, Tod. A last name which has also become popular as a first name, Todd.has two possible meanings—"thicket" (Old English) or "a fox" (Scottish and Norse). Toddy is a nickname.

Tracey, Tracy (Greek, English). This one-time nickname for **Theresa** has become really popular on its own. Like Theresa, your name means "a harvester or reaper" but carries its own meaning, too—"courageous." It has become popular both as a boys' and a girls' name. Nicknames are Trace or Tray. Tennis star Tracy Austin is the youngest player ever to win a major tournament.

Tricia, Trish—see Patricia.

Trina—see Katherine.

Trudy (German). Your name comes from the word *truda,* which means "a maiden." However, it may also be a nickname or a shortened form of the name **Gertrude,** which means "a spear maiden" or "a female warrior." In ancient Norse legends, Gertrude was a Viking warrior who carried the souls of the slain warriors to Valhalla, the Viking heaven. Other ways to spell your name are **Trude** and **Trudie.**

U - V

Ursula (Latin). Your name means " the little she-bear," and it comes from the Latin word *ursa,* which means bear. In the Greek myths, the lovely nymph Callisto was turned into a bear by Hera, the queen of the gods. Callisto was then sent up to the heavens and became a constellation called Ursa Major, or the "Great Bear." You probably know this constellation as the "Big Dipper"! A nickname for Ursula is Ursie.

Valerie (Latin). "Strong and vigorous" are the two meanings of this pretty name. Your name comes from the Latin word *valere,* which means "to be healthy." Valerian is an herb that was often used as a medicine.

This herb is also known as catnip and was considered sacred in ancient Egypt where the cat was highly worshipped. **Valeria** and **Valery** are two other versions of your name, and Val is a popular nickname. In Italy, it's **Valentina** or **Valeria;** in France, **Valérie.**

Vanessa (Greek). This name means "a butterfly," and comes from *phanes,* the Greek word for butterfly. Your name was once spelled **Phanessa.** In the Greek myths, the mysterious Phanessa was a goddess who ruled over a secret brotherhood. There is also a type of butterfly called the phanessa, which is known for its great beauty. Nicknames are Vanny or Van.

Vera (Latin, Russian). "True," "sincere," or "faith" are three possible meanings for this name. Vera may also be a shortened form of **Verity,** a virtue name that was popular in Puritan days. (*Verity* means truthfulness.)

Veronica (Greek). Your name has two possible origins—one is that it first came from the Greek name **Berenice,** which means "a bringer of victory." The second is that your name means "true image" because of Saint Veronica in the Bible. When Veronica dried Jesus' face with a cloth, she saw the exact image of his face on it. Because of this, Saint Veronica has always been known as the patron saint of photographers. In France, your name is spelled **Veronique.** For nicknames you can choose among Nicky, Ronnie, Ronny, or even Bunny.

Victor (Latin). "Victorious," "victory," or "a victor" are meanings of your name which, like its "brother" name **Vincent,** comes from the Latin word *vincere,* meaning "to conquer." Throughout history, Victor has been the name of many popes, kings, and saints. Vic and Vick are the two top nicknames.

Victoria (Latin). Count yourself lucky if this is your name, because it means "victory" and "victorious." Victoria may have originally come from the name **Vincenta,** which means "the conqueror." **Vicki, Vickie,** and **Vikki** are nicknames that are often seen as names on their own. Vic is another short and sweet nickname. Your name first became popular because of Queen Victoria, England's longest reigning queen. She ruled England for a record sixty-four years.

Vincent (Latin). Your name comes from the word *vincere,* which means "to conquer." From Vincent also come the "victory" names **Victoria** and **Victor.** A famous saint was Saint Vincent De Paul, who was known for his efforts to help poor and homeless children. **Vincenta** is the feminine version of your name. Vin, Vinnie, Vinny, and Vince are popular nicknames. Another nickname is—would you believe—Bink?

Viola, **Violet** (Latin). Your name naturally comes from the pretty purple flower called the violet and means "shyness" or "modesty." In fact, someone who is very shy is sometimes called "a shrinking violet." Long ago, singers would receive bunches of violets instead of money as payment for their performances. Other names that have grown out of Violet are **Veola** and **Viette.** You can pick Vi or Vye as nicknames. It's **Violeta** in Italy; and **Violette, Yolette,** or **Yolande** in France.

Virginia (Latin). Virginia originally came from the boys' name **Virgil,** which means "a twig" or "flourishing." The name symbolizes springtime and the new, green, growing things of spring. It used to be a popular name in the American South, probably because of the state of Virginia. Some really neat nicknames come from Virginia—Ginger, Ginny, Ginnie, Virgie, Jinny, and Virg. In France, it's **Virginie;** in Italy, **Virgilia.**

Vivian, Vivien (Latin). Your name means "lively" and "full of life." It used to be that Viv*ian* was mostly a boys' name, and Viv*ien* was the girls' version. Nowadays, however, it's pretty much a girls' name only, no matter how you spell it. **Vita** and **Viva** are two versions of Vivian. Viv is the most common nickname. If you lived in Italy, you might be called **Viviana;** in France, **Vivienne.** Vivian Vance played Ethel Mertz, Lucy's sidekick in the popular TV series, *I Love Lucy.*

Walter (German, Old English). Your name can mean "mighty warrior," "a ruler," "a general," "a master of the forest," "powerful," or "ruler of the host"—take your pick! Wally and Walt are the two top nicknames; but long ago Wat and Watt were nicknames, too. Sir Walter Raleigh was an English soldier and early explorer of America. Walt Whitman was a famous American poet. Walter H. Deubner invented the shopping bag, and Walter Hunt invented the safety pin!

Wanda—see Wendy.

Warren (German). This name means "a game warden" or "a protector of parks." Long ago, a "warren" had the job of guarding the grounds of a large estate against poachers (illegal hunters). Today, game wardens in parks do the same. Some famous Warrens are actor Warren Beatty, former baseball pitcher Warren Spahn, and former U.S. President Warren G. Harding.

Wayne (Old English). Your name means "a wagonmaker" and is actually the shortened version of **Wainwright.** Long ago wainwrights made *wains* (the Old English word for wagon). Wayne is often seen as a last name, as well as a first.

Wendy (German). Do you like to travel? Your name comes from the name **Wandis,** which means "a wanderer." Originally both Wandis and Wendy came from the word "wand" and became associated with shepherds who carry big wands, or crooks, while they tended their sheep. Wendy is also a nickname for **Gwendolyn.** (See **Gwendolyn** for more information.) The most famous Wendy can be found in *Peter Pan.* Other versions of your name are **Wanda, Wendelin,** and **Wenda.**

Wesley (Old English). This is a "residence" name which means "from the west meadow or the west field." **Wesla, Westley,** and **Wellesley** are variations; a favorite nickname is Wes.

William (German). If your name is William, you may be "strong-minded," "determined," or "willful." William originally comes from two German words which mean "will helmet" (*wilhelm*). Because of this, your name has also come to mean a mighty warrior or protector. William is a very popular name. In fact, it's second only to John as one of the all-time most popular names around. Bill, Billy, Will, and Willie are favorite nicknames. William has been the name of many famous people. First there's William the Conqueror, the Norman invader and an ancient warrior who became an English king. Then there's William Shakespeare, the famous playwright. Two Williams of America's Wild West were Wild Bill Hickcock, a gunfighter turned sheriff, and Buffalo Bill Cody, an Indian scout turned performer. Actor William Henry Pratt, better known as Boris Karloff, originated the role of Frankenstein in the movies. Two U.S. presidents were William Howard Taft and William McKinley. Hall of Famer Willie Mays is baseball's "Say-Hey" kid.

Wilma (German). Yours is a shortened form of the name **Wilhelmina.** Wilma can mean "ruler," "warrior," or "protectress"; it can also mean "the willed-for or chosen one." Both names are also related to **William.** Another way to spell this name is **Wylma,** and Willie is a favorite nickname. Track star Wilma Rudolph won three gold medals in the 1960 Olympics; she was voted Woman Athlete of the Year in 1960 and 1961.

Winifred (Welsh, German). This name can either mean "white wave" or "friend of peace." **Winnie,** the most popular nickname, is also an independent name. Other nicknames are Fred, Freddy, and Freddie.

X - Y - Z

Xanthe (Greek). This unusual name means "golden-yellow or golden-haired." It is pronounced "zan-thee." Xanthus was a town in ancient Asia; it was known for its beautiful, golden-haired women.

Yvonne, **Yvette** (French). Both names are feminine forms of **Yves** ("eeve"). Yves originally came from the Scandinavian name **Iver,** meaning "an archer or bowman."

Zachary, **Zach** (Hebrew). Your name is next to last on the list, but definitely not least! It means "God has remembered" and was originally spelled **Zachariah.** Zachary was a popular name during America's pioneer days. Zach is a favorite nickname as well as a popular name in its own right. **Zack** is another way to spell it. President Zachary Taylor helped to make your name popular. His nickname was "Old Rough and Ready."

Zöe (Greek). This pretty name is closely related to Eve, and its meaning is the same: "life." Although it's usually pronounced "zo-ee," the ancient Greeks pronounced the name to rhyme with "joy." Lucky you—you're bound to have a "life of joy"—if your name is Zöe!